EXHUMING FRANCO

EXHUMING FRANCO

Spain's Second Transition

SEBASTIAAN FABER

VANDERBILT UNIVERSITY PRESS
Nashville, Tennessee

Library of Congress Cataloging-in-Publication Data

Names: Faber, Sebastiaan, 1969– author.
Title: Exhuming Franco : Spain's second transition / Sebastiaan
    Faber.
Description: Nashville : Vanderbilt University Press, [2021] |
    Includes bibliographical references and index.
Identifiers: LCCN 2020055861 (print) | LCCN 2020055862
    (ebook) | ISBN 9780826501738 (paperback) | ISBN
    9780826501745 (epub) | ISBN 9780826501752 (pdf)
Subjects: LCSH: Franco, Francisco, 1892–1975—Influence. |
    Spain—Politics and government—1982– | Intellectuals—
    Spain—Interviews. | Collective memory—Spain. | Exhuma-
    tion—Spain—History—21st century.
Classification: LCC DP264.F7 F25 2021 (print) | LCC DP264.
    F7 (ebook) | DDC 946.084—dc23

LC record available at https://lccn.loc.gov/2020055861
LC ebook record available at https://lccn.loc.gov/2020055862

To Kim, Jakob, and Maya

CONTENTS

INTRODUCTION
Securely Tied Down

If it hadn't been for a couple of straps and last-minute screws, the embalmed corpse of Francisco Franco may well have slipped from its coffin and crashed onto the esplanade. The scene—macabre and surrealist, with the entire world looking on—would have been worthy of Luis Buñuel. Fortunately for Franco, things happened otherwise.

A bit before one o'clock in the afternoon on October 24, 2019, eight pallbearers carefully carried the former dictator's remains out of the basilica at the Valley of the Fallen, toward the hearse that had pulled up a short distance away. Peeking out from under a brown cloth covering the coffin were two bright orange straps that kept the entire thing together. Just moments earlier, when Franco's tombstone was lifted, it had become clear that forty-four years under ground had left their mark: the coffin had suffered serious water damage. Because the wood had decayed in several places, the funeral experts who were supervising the operation recommended transferring the dictator's remains to a new container. Yet the family members present, who had been opposed to the exhumation until the very end, rejected that idea out of hand. ("Here we are, grandpa," Franco's grand-daughter had groused a moment before. "Here we are, with these defilers of your grave!") (Escolar and Ejerique 2019).

The experts refused to give any guarantees. Still, the rickety coffin had to be moved, so they put in a couple of screws to strengthen its rotten corners and strapped it on to a large wooden plank that they happened to have on hand. The emergency measures worked: the coffin made it to the hearse without incident, and from there into a helicopter. Moments later, Franco's remains—straps and all—had arrived at the family plot, a short twenty-mile flight from the Valley. There, the brown cloth covering the coffin was replaced with a Francoist flag while a priest—who, as it happened, was the son of the officer who in 1981 had led a failed military coup—issued a homily in which he praised the dictator as a great leader and champion of Catholicism. Finally, the Generalissimo was reinterred next to his wife.

Franco, who ruled Spain from his 1939 victory in the Span-ish Civil War until his death in 1975, wasn't known for his sense of humor. Still, he might have appreciated the sym-bolism of those unsightly orange straps. "Todo ha quedado atado, bien atado," he famously said in his 1969 Christmas address to the nation: "Everything is tied down, securely tied down." The phrase described his intended legacy. That same summer, Juan Carlos de Borbón, the grandson of Spain's last king, had sworn loyalty to the principles of Francoism, after which the parliament had appointed him as Franco's successor. The continuation of the regime was secure, the then seventy-seven-year-old dictator assured his listeners—even after his eventual death.

Has Franco been able to keep his posthumous promise? Does he continue to exert power from beyond the grave? How many of Spain's challenges today can be ascribed to Franco's legacies? These are questions that continue to divide Spaniards five decades on. Around the time of the exhumation, which coincided with the conflict over Catalonia's bid for independence, Spain's social-democratic caretaker government launched a campaign to reinforce the country's image at home and abroad. Through tweets, videos, and events, Spain was presented as a "consolidated democracy": "one of the freest and safest countries" in the world, with a rule of law that's among the globe's "most advanced." Yet many Spaniards dare to disagree, including a good part of the Left and large sectors of Catalonia and the Basque Country. In their eyes, Spanish democracy is anything but consolidated. If anything, it is dangerously fragile, with its longtime Francoist substratum on the rise rather than in retreat. The results of the two parliamentary elections that took place in April and November 2019 seem to confirm this impression. In April, the Far-Right party Vox—which embraces Spanish nationalism, rejects "gender ideology" and "the dictatorship of political correctness," idolizes the imperial past, wants to "make Spain great again," and defends citizens' right to proudly celebrate Franco's regime—entered parliament for the first time, with some 10 percent of the vote (24 of the 350 available seats). By November, Vox had expanded its share of the electoral pie to over 15 percent and more than doubled its number of deputies.

And Vox is only the tip of Spain's Francoist iceberg, the journalist Emilio Silva assured me not long before the exhumation. "Our democracy has dragged Franco's heavy tombstone around its neck for years," he said. "Francoism is deeply ingrained in Spain's political culture." Silva is the founder of the Association for the Recovery of Historical Memory (Asociación para la Recuperación de la Memoria Histórica, or ARMH), a grassroots civil-society initiative that for the past twenty years has applied pressure on the country's governments to settle the many *cuentas pendientes*— the unfinished business—left over from the Franco years. Since the ARMH's creation in 2000, its teams of volunteers have located and exhumed hundreds of mass graves with thousands of victims, most of whom died at the hands of military and paramilitary supporters of the Nationalists in the Spanish Civil War. The ARMH took the initiative where the Spanish government hasn't dared to.

Ironically, the largest mass grave in the country is, of all places, the Valley of the Fallen, which is estimated to hold the remains of more than thirty thousand Spaniards. Its construction was begun in 1940; it was inaugurated in 1959, by Franco himself, on the twentieth anniversary of his successful victory in the civil war. "How could I express the profound emotion that overcomes us in the presence of the mothers and wives of our Fallen," he had said in an emotional speech, "represented by these exemplary women who are here today, and who, fully aware of their Fatherlands' demands, one day draped medals around their [sons' and husbands'] necks and encouraged them to fight?"

Our war was evidently not just another civil war but a true Crusade, as the Pope called it at the time: the great epic struggle for a new . . . independence. . . . The entire evolution of our Crusade was marked by providence and miracles. How else to describe the decisive help we received on so many occasions from our divine protector? . . . The anti-Spain was conquered and defeated, but it hasn't died yet. Periodically we see it raise its head abroad as it tries, in its arrogance and blindness, to poison our youth and encourage in it, once more, its innate curiosity and thirst for new things. This is why it is necessary to close ranks against the diversion of the bad educators of the new generations. (Franco 1959)

That same day, the body of José Antonio Primo de Rivera, the founder of Spanish fascism who had been executed by the Republicans in 1936, was moved to the Valley. So were the remains of thousands of others who'd died during the war. (This transfer often happened without the families' consent, as Montse Armengou and Ricard Belis revealed in a 2013 documentary on the topic.) Sixteen years later, Franco's body was buried alongside Primo de Rivera's, in the center of the massive nave.

Over the years, the Valley has remained practically unchanged. In addition to a basilica and esplanade, the site features a Benedictine abbey, whose members still celebrate a daily Catholic mass. Because the Valley is a public monument, it's maintained with taxpayer money—with significant funds laid out in recent years to slow down its decay—over the objections of citizens like Silva, who think it's an affront that a democratic state should fund the upkeep of a monument that glorifies fascism. The Valley has been a shrine for Franco nostalgics, but also for the dictator's enemies. Jack Shafran, an American who fought as a volunteer soldier against Franco in the Spanish Civil War, swore an oath while facing a particularly heavy bombardment during the war. If he survived, he told himself, he'd return someday "to piss on Franco's grave." In 1986, he had a chance to visit the Valley of the Fallen. Before heading out, he entered a pharmacy and purchased a glass vial, which he took to his hotel room. He filled the vial with urine, stuck it in his pocket, and emptied it on the tomb when the guard looked away (Volunteer 2003).

For Pedro Sánchez, the leader of the social-democratic PSOE, the Valley presented a welcome opportunity to prove his progressive credentials when, in the summer of 2018, he became prime minister after a successful vote of no confidence against Mariano Rajoy, the leader of the conservative Partido Popular (PP). Less than three weeks after taking office, Sánchez announced his intention to remove Franco's body from the monument. "Spain can no longer afford to have symbols that divide the country," he said in a television interview. He also announced that the Valley would become "a memorial for the struggle against fascism" and a site of "reconciliation." In September, the Spanish parliament approved the measure; the vote passed with support from Spain's progressive parties and the Catalan and Basque nationalists, while the two main conservative parties, Rajoy's PP and Ciudadanos (Citizens), abstained. Still, their disdain for the measure was clear. The PP accused Sánchez of playing politics with symbols in an attempt to rally his base. Meanwhile, the Franco family, which still wields considerable power in Spain, took to the courts to try to stop the exhumation. This effort failed, and the reburial finally took place on October 24, 2019, once the Supreme Court had cleared the way. The moment could not have been more politically tense: the previous week had seen the controversial conviction, by the same Supreme Court, of nine Catalan independence leaders; a bit over two weeks later, Spaniards went to the polls to vote in parliamentary elections for the second time that year.

That Franco's controversial exhumation overflowed with symbolism was clear. But what exactly it symbolized was subject to divergent interpretations. "Today, Spain has fulfilled a promise to itself," Sánchez declared triumphantly. "With this, a moral shame—which is what extolling a dictator in a public space is—finally comes to an end." Here and there, champagne corks popped. The Right cried foul. Yet the way in which the Sánchez government had approached the operation also garnered criticism from the Left. "This could have been a great day for Franco's victims," the journalist Antonio Maestre wrote in the magazine *La Marea*. "Instead, it was an embarrassing display" (2019b). Not only had the government granted the Franco family an inappropriately central role in the whole affair—they were allowed to carry the coffin, covered with a wreath—but the sheer solemnity of the ceremony, in the presence of a Minister of Justice, amounted to a slap in the face of the dictator's victims. Maestre's indignation was shared broadly.

The controversy surrounding Franco's exhumation also fanned the flames of a militant Spanish nationalism that reemerged with force in 2017, following Catalonia's attempt to declare independence. It was this wave that, in April 2019, carried Vox, the young party on the Far Right, into the national parliament. Although not all Spanish nationalists are nostalgic for Franco, the Right's radical core undoubtedly is. In July 2018, for example, the "Movement for Spain" organized a "pilgrimage" to Franco's grave to protest the government's plans for the Valley. "Half of Spain is opposed to the exhumation of Franco and the profanation and pillaging of the Valley of the Fallen," the movement's leaders warned. Images from the gathering showed groups brandishing Francoist flags, their hands raised in the fascist salute. And the flirtation with fascism is not limited to symbolic gestures. An official state poll from December 2019 revealed that some 21 percent of the 3.7 million Vox voters agreed with the statement: "In some circumstances, an authoritarian government is preferable to a democratic system" (ElPlural 2020).

Spain's parliamentary monarchy is reaching middle age. The current Constitution, which was approved by referendum in 1978, resulted from a negotiation between the Franco regime and the democratic opposition. The country entered the European Community, now European Union, in 1986, four years after joining NATO, and its successive governments have liked to boast that Spain is a "consolidated democracy." Still, no one who has been following the news in recent years can deny that there is plenty of room for improvement. In fact, what a recent editorial in the magazine *Contexto* called "los fallos del sistema," the system's structural flaws, have been the focus of constant political debate at least since the mass protests of May 2011 known as the 15M or the *indignados* movement (CTXT 2020). The

15M was a broad mobilization of civil society—initially sparked by the austerity policies imposed in response to the Great Recession—that denounced the "regime of 1978" as closed, corrupt, and undemocratic. "No nos representan" the protestors chanted ("They do not represent us"), calling for "democracia real, ¡ya!" ("real democracy, now!").

In the years that followed it, the 15M inspired the creation of new political parties such as Podemos, whose rapid rise broke open what until then had largely been a two-party system, at least at the national level. Within only a couple of years, Spain's political landscape changed beyond recognition. Podemos's success at the ballot box only months after its foundation in early 2014 sent shock waves through the system; among other things, it prompted King Juan Carlos I to hurriedly abdicate in favor of his son, Felipe VI, less than a week later. In May 2015, politicians allied with Podemos won municipal elections in several of the country's largest cities, including Madrid and Barcelona; later that year, the party entered the national parliament. By early 2020, Podemos and the social-democratic PSOE formed the first progressive coalition government Spain has seen since the 1930s.

Ironically, the threat to the establishment posed by the political newcomers who denounced the dysfunctions of Spanish democracy exacerbated those very dysfunctions, at least initially, as the economic and political elites fought tooth and nail to preserve their power and privilege. At the same time, the widening cracks in the existing structures—not only in politics but also in the media and the judiciary—have opened spaces for new actors who are not afraid to break long-standing taboos and expose systemic corruption in all spheres of Spanish society.

And expose they did. Over the past decade, the Spanish public sphere has been inundated with examples large and small of kickback schemes, power abuse, judicial malfeasance, and forms of social and economic inequality that many would consider unacceptable in a modern democracy. A montage of headlines selected more or less at random would include the case of a public university president caught plagiarizing on a massive scale; several prominent politicians boasting academic degrees that were gifted to them as political favors; the conservative party financing its election campaigns, and enriching its leadership, for decades through systematic corporate bribes; puppeteers, rappers, and comedians brought up on charges of terrorism for the content of their shows, lyrics, and jokes; a prominent judge disbarred after he dared to investigate crimes against humanity committed during the dictatorship; a member of the royal family found guilty of corruption but treated with extraordinary leniency by the courts; a group of young adults in the Basque Country jailed for terrorism after a bar fight with off-duty military police; or the discovery of a longstanding network of journalists, cabinet members, and high-ranking police chiefs conspiring to leak false police reports in order to slander political rivals.

As a result of these revelations—and the near-total lack of accountability of those involved—citizens' levels of trust in the political system, the monarchy, the judiciary, the university, the press, and other central democratic institutions have sunk to new lows. When a nationwide poll in April 2019 asked voters to grade political party leaders on a 1 to 10 scale, not a single one got even close to a passing grade (Junquera 2019). According to a spring 2019 poll conducted by the European Union, 55 percent of Spaniards gave a negative rating when asked about the independence of the country's judiciary, leaving Spain ranked the fourth lowest in the EU (Vanguardia 2019a; European Commission 2019a). And although the state-level polling authority has not dared to ask Spaniards about the monarchy for years, other polls indicate that barely half of the country supports it (Gay 2019). Discontent with the royal family is particularly high in regions such as Catalonia and the Basque Country, where around three quarters of the population favors a republican form of government—and where the right-wing parties associated with Spanish nationalism and the monarchy have seen their electoral base erode. Another 2019 EU-wide poll measuring the population's trust in their national government put Spain, once again, at fourth from the bottom (European Commission 2019b), while a national poll in early 2020 indicated that more than half of the population considered politicians and their behavior to be the country's most serious problem (Aduriz 2020).

How to frame this discontent is itself a deeply political question. In both Spain and abroad, critics often point to the system's dysfunctions and the resulting lack of legitimacy as symptoms of a structural problem whose origins lie in the country's recent history. In this interpretation, Spain's current problems are tell-tale signs of the fact that Spain's transition to democracy, long upheld as an international example, is in fact still very much a work in progress—if it's not a lost cause altogether. A reader's reaction to a January 2020 column by Rosa María Artal in *ElDiario.es*, one of the country's largest online newspapers, is representative of this trend:

Spain is a democracy but a very special one. Our democracy is the result of an "adaptation maneuver" by
the regime of General Franco when it was faced with
the choice to either integrate into Europe or maintain
itself in indefinite isolation. Its master move was to force
a Transition in which those who held power during the
dictatorship remained in place, concealed under the cloak
of a democratic society.

At that moment, there may have been no opportunity to achieve something more presentable, given the
strength of the Right. Yet a couple of years later, during
the successive majority governments of Felipe González
[of the Socialist Party], a golden opportunity was lost to
turn this country inside out like a sock. But the PSOE
of *felipismo* was not up to the task. They preferred to
institute some more or less superficial improvements,
without touching the "hard core" of Francoist power
still lurking in every single state institution. We'll never
have an opportunity like that again.

All the political problems that we suffer from today
derive from those two historical facts: the true objective
of our "less-than-exemplary Transition" and the lack of
ambition for renewal of Felipe González's four governments. . . . It's a mistake for which we'll surely pay very
dearly! (Osiris 2020)

This history-driven reading of the political present is
widespread, and not only among the Left. The Basques and
Catalans who favor independence from Spain—a position
that straddles the left/right divide—also like to portray the
Spanish state as a Trojan horse of Francoist values. "We did

not embark on the process toward independence only to change a couple of minor details," the former Catalan president Carles Puigdemont, a lifelong member of a conservative party, said when Gijs Mulder and I interviewed him in 2018: "We are sick and tired of having to call for an end to the Francoist legacy. Instead, what we see is the renewal of a duchy granted by Franco, the continued legality of the Franco Foundation, a disgraceful debate over Franco's exhumation. . . . It's all so tiresome and frustrating. We just want to leave all that behind" (Faber and Mulder 2018).

While they portray the Spanish state as a repository of Francoism, the Catalan and Basque independence movements see themselves as engines of democratic renewal. During the investiture debate in January 2020 that led to the country's first coalition government since the 1930s, the Basque deputy Mertxe Aizpurua of the pro-independence party EH Bildu underscored the crucial role that the regional independence movements play in the evolution of Spanish democracy. "There will be no advanced democratic model available to the [Spanish] state unless it's with the support of the *independentistas*," she said. "Unless we apply the democratizing agenda of *soberanismo* [the belief in the right to regional self-determination], there will be no break with the legacy of the dictator whose body you removed from the Valley of the Fallen last October" (RTVE 2020).

In parliament and outside of it, statements like these are met with scorn and indignation by the Madrid-based political and media establishment. The idea that the Spanish state in its current form suffers from a stubbornly persistent Francoism belies Spanish elites' long-held aspiration to European "normality"—a key concept in what has since become known as "the Culture of the Transition" (Delgado 2014; Martínez 2012). For the critics, by contrast, Spain is the exact opposite of normal. For all its protestations to the contrary, they say, in the Western European landscape Spain continues to stand out like a sore thumb. Every time a politician or university administrator survives yet another embarrassing revelation of abuse, corruption, or plagiarism, pundits are quick to point out that if they'd been German, French, or British, they would have been forced to resign long ago.

To be sure, this critical view relies on an idealized version of the Northern European countries, whose own democracies face plenty of challenges. Still, the critics have a point. If we consider the lack of accountability among Spanish politicians and others in positions of power who have been accused or found guilty of wrongdoing; the persistently low rankings of Spanish universities; the weakness of professional ethics in the media; or even the fact that praising Franco and his legacy is not illegal in Spain while extolling Nazism and fascism is proscribed by law elsewhere in Europe, then yes, Spain continues to be "different," to invoke the notorious tourist slogan from the 1960s. It's no surprise, then, that the call for a "second transition" has been growing stronger by the year. But it's one thing to point to Spain's political problems and another to explain them almost exclusively as consequences of the Franco dictatorship and the Transition.

Why has it been so tempting for many to interpret Spain's social and political challenges as proof of an unprocessed Francoist legacy? How useful is that narrative as an analytical or explanatory paradigm? If the goal is to improve the quality of Spanish democracy, how important is it that its deficiencies be identified as remnants from the dictatorship? And even if it's true that Spanish democracy can't advance until it comes to terms with its past, can't the same be said of many other countries, including the United States? What might the rest of the world learn from the Spanish case? These are the questions that inform this short book.

Opinions are divided, even among the Left. For Emilio Silva, the leading figure in the grassroots movement defending the rights of Franco's victims I mentioned earlier, Francoism is still very much "part of [Spain's] political culture." It is this persistence, he argued in 2019, that explains the systemic fragility of Spanish democracy and the excessive politicization of the entire state apparatus, from the judiciary and the educational system to the media and the foreign service.

Ignacio Echevarría, a prominent literary critic, doesn't see things in quite the same way. "The remnants of Francoism, for all their visibility, are not the main problem of Spanish society—far from it," he wrote in the magazine *Contexto* a month after Franco's exhumation. Those critics that claim the contrary, he added, are caught in a misperception. The phenomena they denounce as traces of Francoism "in part date from much earlier and in part are radically new." That's even true for the Far-Right party Vox, Echevarría added, some of whose supporters appear openly nostalgic of the dictatorship. "It would appear," Echevarría wrote, "that the Francoist pedigree of a significant part of the Spanish Right . . . marks some kind of fundamental difference between it and the rest of the European Right." But the reality is different. In practice, "the underpinnings and interests

of the Spanish Right . . . are the same as those of the Right
in the entire rest of the world." In fact, Echevarría added,
"many representatives of Spanish neoliberalism have little
or nothing to do with Francoism and profess a solid faith
in representative democracy" (2019).

True, Echevarría admitted, the designers of Spain's Transition may have neglected to eliminate Francoism and its
symbols from public life. But that doesn't change the fact
that "Francoism, like fascism, . . . is today a thing of the
past." This is key. Because those who refuse to accept this
basic fact are committing a serious political mistake. "To
attribute the rise of a Spanish Far Right to a resurgence of
a latent Francoism rather than an almost inevitable assimi-
lation of certain sectors of Spanish society with right-wing
neo-populism, which is so vigorous in France or Italy, is
not only misleading and erroneous. For those who consider
themselves to be on the Left, it is a failure to acknowledge
the true nature of the 'enemy'" (2019).

So, which is it? Do Francoist legacies continue to shape
Spain today, or did most of the country, including its right
wing, move on long ago? The answer to that question—
which, as I said, is the main one driving this book—depends on how one defines those legacies. In what follows,
I will refer to Francoism not merely as a political cause or
ideology embraced—openly or covertly—by part of the
Spanish Right, as Echevarría does. Rather, following Silva, I
will define it in a broader sense: as a series of ideas, attitudes,
institutions, narratives, social relations, legal structures, and
practices that may still be discernible across Spanish society.

To any objective observer, it's clear that Spain today is
unrecognizably different from what it was at any point

during Franco's almost forty-year rule. Apart from the simple fact that it's a parliamentary democracy and member of the European Union, Spain has also been at the vanguard of progressive causes, from the innovative deployment of universal jurisdiction to prosecute human rights violations to the legalization of same-sex marriage. International rankings and statistics routinely place Spain among the most advanced democracies of the world. The 2019 Democracy Index compiled by the Economist Intelligence Unit ranked Spain at 16, ahead of France, and as one of the world's 24 "full democracies" (EIU 2019). On the other hand, it's also important to acknowledge that Francoism did not appear out of nowhere; it emerged from, and helped unify, reactionary organizations, projects, and ideologies that go back at least to the nineteenth century—and that are not exclusive to Spain, either. "Francoism didn't actually invent much," the historian Jaume Claret told me. "It simply took advantage of its totalitarian power to grant pride of place to the ultra-conservative strain of Spanish right-wing political thought, at the expense of liberalism and Christian democracy, the Right's other two principal currents."

Although in many ways Spain today looks nothing like it did between 1939 and 1975, Francoism as an *explanatory paradigm* is still remarkably popular among broad segments of the population and intellectual class. Many Spanish and foreign observers assume that Spain's successes and failures, its deficiencies and points of pride, can only be understood *through* Francoism. Perhaps surprisingly, this tendency straddles the political spectrum. For some, especially on the Right, the relationship to the country's dictatorial past is best understood in providential terms. In this view, even

Spain's current democracy is paradoxically one of Franco's many valuable gifts to the nation. Others, especially on the Left, see the relationship to the Francoist period in terms of unfinished business, in a moral, judicial, economic, or political sense. For yet others, who, as we saw, include many of those who aspire to Basque or Catalan independence, Francoism functions also as a destiny of sorts, but in negative terms. In this view, the dictator's legacy operates like a malignant curse. Spain is *irreformable* because it's been irremediably infected with the Francoist virus, an imperialist thrust whose origins long preceded the dictatorship. The only way to kill it is to destroy the Spanish state altogether—or at least move beyond it (Gabilondo 2014, 2019b).

Why, we might wonder, is this explanatory paradigm still so popular? Could its very persistence—the temptation, that is, to read current problems as traces of an improperly processed past, a virus, or curse—itself be a legacy of Francoism? Franco, after all, identified himself fully with the destiny of the Spanish nation, which he consistently defined in exceptionalist terms. He also presented himself as a providential leader, whose hard hand was necessary for a country afflicted with an unruly and fratricidal national character. Ironically, it is in this stubborn identification of Spain with Francoism where the Far Right coincides with some of the most critical sectors of the Left.

Franco's embrace of Spanish exceptionalism, nationalism, and imperialism fueled his obsession with Spain's international status. Francoist propaganda and textbooks portrayed Spain as a providential nation, the "spiritual guide of the world," chosen by God himself to save the rest of humanity. Although few people today beyond the far religious

Right defend this notion, the concern with Spain's status in the world continues to feature centrally in public discourse. In recent years, in fact, it has served to fuel a wave of revisionist history. Leading the pack is Elvira Roca Barea, a high school history teacher from Andalusia with two best-selling books: *Imperiofobia y leyenda negra* (2016; Phobia of empire and black legend) and *Fracasología: España y sus elites* (2019; Failurology: Spain and its elites). According to Roca Barea, for the past two hundred years Spain's intellectual elites have done their country a great disservice by swallowing hook, line, and sinker the critical views of Spanish history spread by the country's international rivals. These rivals, she argues, have consistently painted the actions of Spaniards in too negative a light—whether it's regarding the Inquisition, the fifteenth-century expulsion of Jews and Muslims, the colonization of the Americas, the Enlightenment, or the bloody conflicts of the twentieth century.

Some of Roca Barea's tenets have seeped into official government discourse. When the social-democratic government launched its campaign to reinforce Spain's democratic image in 2019, Irene Lozano, the junior minister in charge of the operation, suggested that anyone who doubts the quality of the country's democracy plays into the hand of "Spain's enemies." By invoking this phrase—which was also one of Franco's favorites—Lozano was referring to Spain's historical rivals, including England, the United States, and the Netherlands, but also the Catalan and Basque independence movements, which, as we saw, like to paint the Spanish central state as retrograde, inefficient, and authoritarian.

If Pedro Sánchez decided to go ahead with Franco's solemn exhumation, it was undoubtedly in part because he believed it would serve to improve this negative international image. But the irony was a bit too obvious. Exhumations, after all, have been at the center of the debate about Spain's incomplete transition to democracy. It has been precisely the Spanish government's unwillingness to take charge of the mass graves of the thousands of victims of right-wing violence that, for the past twenty years, has fueled calls for a "second Transition." Viewed from a broader perspective, removing the dead dictator amounted to little more than an aesthetic gesture, much like getting rid of an old couch that ruined the look of a living room while ignoring the cracks in the foundation. Franco's exhumation did nothing for the family members of the disappeared, who have been asking the government for decades to assume its duty—a duty imposed by international law—and help them locate and rebury the remains of their loved ones. A new Law of Democratic Memory, proposed in September 2020, may address these concerns. But will a change in the government's attitude with regard to the mass graves be enough? If Spain needs to come to terms with its past in order to move on, what would that "coming to terms" look like exactly? Should there be a truth commission, as representatives of the United Nations have suggested? These are questions we'll get to in the last couple of chapters.

Speaking of chapters, a brief note on structure and style. This book was born in dialogue. I have benefited enormously from the work of friends and colleagues in Spain with whom I have been discussing these issues for years. Between December 2019 and May 2020, some twenty-five individuals agreed to answer, in writing or in person, an additional set of questions specifically formulated for this project. A handful of others sat down with me, in person or over the phone, for more extensive interviews. It was important for me to integrate all these views and voices into the text; the style, for that reason, is more journalistic than academic. This makes this book quite hybrid and multivoiced but also, I hope, quite readable, although the format comes with some drawbacks as well. For one, the dialogic, spoken structure of the interview, while increasing readability, lends itself less well to the pondered, distant rhetorical position of the scholarly observer. The limited length and the journalistic style of the book also mean that it has less bibliographical breadth and depth than a regular scholarly monograph would. To give readers a better sense of the bibliography available without losing the accessibility of the format, I include brief suggestions for further reading where appropriate.

Some of my informants are journalists, while others are academics or members of the creative classes. All have lived in Spain for a significant part of their lives. Still, although my selection of interlocutors reflects a wide range of views, it is not representative in a strictly proportional sense. Nor is it meant to be. The reason for this is simple: the debate about the questions driving this book has been more intense, interesting, and varied among the Left than among the Right. While most of the individuals I spoke to would identify as progressive rather than conservative, they still disagree on fundamental points.

Arranged as a series of snapshots, the chapters shift back and forth between analysis, reportage, and full-length interviews. The chapter following this introduction returns to the moment of exhumation and then jumps back in time to give a rather brisk overview of recent Spanish history. Chapter 2 considers the many and often surreptitious ways in which a form of "sociological Francoism" may have survived beyond the dictator's death. It is followed by two interviews on those same topics: with the literary critic Ignacio Echevarría, who inspired some of the central questions informing this book, and with the journalist Guillem Martínez. Chapters 5 through 13 consider the traces of Francoism in different spheres of Spanish society, from the media and parliamentary politics to the economy and the judiciary. The three interviews that make up Chapters 14, 15, and 16 reflect explicitly on two frequently floated demands associated with a "second Transition": a truth commission and a national museum of the Civil War and Francoism. The conclusion, finally, returns to the main questions outlined in this introduction to suggest that the challenges Spain faces may be less different than we think from those confronted by other countries, including the United States.

Parts of this book revise and rework material from articles that have appeared elsewhere. Sections of this introduction rework a piece that came out in Dutch in *De Groene Amsterdammer* (Faber 2019a). The interview with Ignacio Echevarría in Chapter 3 appeared in Spanish, in the magazine *Contexto*, in February 2020. Part of Chapter 9 incorporates a rewritten section from a review essay that came out in *Public Books* (Faber 2017). For part of Chapter 12, I rely on the reporting that Bécquer Seguín and I have done for *The Nation* magazine (2015), some of which in turn made it into a co-authored essay for a collection edited by Steven Torres and Óscar Pereiro-Zazo and published by Palgrave

(Faber and Seguín 2019). All these materials are reproduced with permission.

In the year or so that has passed since I spoke with my informants, Spain has been among the countries hardest hit by the COVID-19 pandemic. But this hasn't stopped the memory battles and the debate over Franco's legacy—to the contrary. In early September 2020, a court ruling returned to the public domain a large manor that had passed into the dictator's real estate portfolio and was still owned by his family. Later that same month, Prime Minister Pedro Sánchez's cabinet approved a Law of Democratic Memory, meant to complement a similar law dating from 2007 and to meet the long-standing demands for justice and recognition of thousands of victims of the Franco dictatorship. The new law, whose parliamentary approval is still pending as this book goes to press, would provide material and symbolic reparations for victims of state violence and theft; open the door to an annulment of judicial sentences from sham courts designed to eliminate Franco's political dissidents; reform public history education; limit freedom of speech for antidemocratic ideologies; and remove or prohibit public tributes to the dictatorship. If passed, the consequences of the law could be far-reaching. In addition to acknowledging that the state is responsible for locating and exhuming the tens of thousands of mass graves dating from the war and the dictatorship—a task that, until now, has been taken on by families and volunteers—the law calls for an inventory of illicit transfers of property and wealth during the war and the Franco regime. It also seeks to issue some form of

reparation to the thousands of Spaniards who did "peni-
tence" for their political "sins" in forced-labor battalions
that, in addition to bridges, roads, and dams, helped build
the Valley of the Fallen (Faber and Seguín 2020).

Some have celebrated the law, although many admit
that its measures are shamefully overdue. Others think that
the proposed draft doesn't go far enough. Most glaringly,
it leaves untouched the Amnesty Law that forces Franco's
victims to seek justice in international courts, a story told
in the award-winning documentary *El silencio de otros* (Carracedo and Bahar, dirs., 2018; *The Silence of Others* [2019]). Predictably, the proposal incensed the Spanish Right, which
accused Spain's progressive government, once again, of
breaking the pact that enabled the country's transition to
democracy. Following the example of their European and
US counterparts, Spain's conservative leaders hope to spin
electoral wool by demonizing antifascism. In Spain, this
means questioning the legitimacy of the Left's decades-
long resistance against the Franco dictatorship, which included different forms of armed struggle. In response to
the proposed law, one deputy from the conservative Partido Popular wrote that it's a "fallacy" to identify anti-
Francoism with democracy (Álvarez de Toledo 2020). In
October 2020, the city government of Madrid—ruled by
the Right with the support of the Far-Right Vox—voted to
remove a memorial plaque to Francisco Largo Caballero, a
longtime socialist union leader. (A Republican prime minister during the civil war, Largo Caballero was later arrested
by the Gestapo, interrogated by Klaus Barbie, and deported
to a Nazi concentration camp; he survived the war but
died in exile soon after.) Ironically, the city government

defended its decision by invoking the 2007 memory law, which prohibits extolling individuals who participated in the failed military coup that unleashed the civil war or in the Francoist repression. In a throwback to old Francoist arguments, City Hall argued that it was the radicalism of leftist leaders like Largo Caballero that stoked much of the political violence in the first place.

FURTHER READING

For a detailed critical take on Roca Barea's work, see Villacañas (2019) and Straehle (2019). Encarnación (2014, 2020) provides an excellent social-scientific analysis of Spain's democratic transition, challenging the conventional wisdom that memory and justice are indispensable for a healthy democracy to emerge out of a dictatorship. For a more critical view of the dynamics of memory and forgetting in the Transition, see Aguilar (2002), Izquierdo Martín and Sánchez León (2006), and Aguilar and Payne (2016). A short, more up-to-date account of the Transition, also by a political scientist, is by Sánchez-Cuenca (2020). Among the strongest voices among the moderate Left who have defended the Transition from a liberal interpretation of Spanish history are historians like Juliá (2017) and Shubert and Álvarez Junco (2000). A positive read on the Transition can also be found in the biography of Adolfo Suárez by Fuentes (2011), especially its Epilogue.

I

How Dead Is He?

"Our top story tonight: Generalissimo Francisco Franco is still dead," Chevy Chase deadpanned on December 13, 1975, in his Weekend Update on *Saturday Night Live.* The show—then still *NBC's Saturday Night*—had premiered only two months before and the Spanish dictator, who had ruled Spain since 1939, became a running gag throughout its first and second seasons. In fact, it seems that the Generalissimo was posthumously adopted as an honorary member of that year's cast, alongside John Belushi, Gilda Radner, and Dan Ackroyd. When producer Lorne Michaels published the first collection of the show's gags and scripts, in 1977, it was Franco who appeared on the cover, in a colorized photograph, as "host."

Three weeks earlier, on November 22, Chase had first informed his viewers of the death of the eighty-two-year-old Spanish head of state, whose failing health had been in the news for weeks. "Reactions from world leaders were varied," Chase said. "Held in contempt as the last of the fascist dictators in the West by some, he was also eulogized by others, among them Richard Nixon, who said. . ."—at this point, the slide behind Chase switched to a photograph of Franco alongside Adolf Hitler, with the arm of the Spanish leader lifted in a Nazi salute—"*Franco was a loyal friend and ally of the United States. He earned worldwide respect for Spain through firmness and fairness.*" The ironic contrast between text and image perfectly captured Franco's evolution from shadow member of the Axis before and during World War II to anti-Communist "sentinel of the West" in the years of the Cold War. "Despite Franco's death and an expected burial tomorrow," Chase concluded, "doctors say the dictator's health has taken a turn for the worse."

Forty-five years later, the *SNL* skit has lost little of its punch or, for that matter, relevance. Franco is still dead, of course; but he also continues to be held in contempt, to garner praise, and to dominate the headlines. Over the past forty-four years, the Spanish Far Right has openly celebrated his legacy on the anniversary of his passing, with Catholic masses in his honor, multitudinous meetings at the Plaza de Oriente in Madrid, and flag-waving gatherings at Franco's grave. In 2002, the conservative government of Prime Minister José María Aznar caused a stir when it awarded a state subsidy to the Franco Foundation, which is dedicated to promoting the dictator's legacy. In 2005, Far-Right groups protested the removal of an equestrian statue of the former head-of-state in Madrid that had been left untouched for decades. In 2015, the historian Ángel Viñas revealed that Franco, who cultivated a public image of modesty, moderation, and austerity, had taken shameless advantage of the civil war and his close to four decades of autocratic rule to enrich himself and his family to a perverse extent (Viñas 2015). Today, the Franco clan holds assets that some estimates put at $550 million (Torrús 2017).

If these incidents can be chalked up as relatively minor episodes, Franco's ghost has at other moments shaken the very bedrock of the Spanish state. In 2008, the investigative judge Baltasar Garzón scandalized conservative public opinion and the judicial establishment when he formally requested the General's death certificate as he prepared to investigate crimes against humanity committed under his rule. A bold, unprecedented attempt to implement international law on domestic soil, Garzón's intervention, which had been prompted by victims of the dictatorship, also questioned the foundational principles and master narrative of Spain's young democracy. But the system swiftly closed ranks and Garzón's adventure would eventually result in his disbarment.

As we saw, in the summer of 2018, the Spanish government headed by the social democrat Pedro Sánchez decided it was time to remove the dictator from his all too conspicuous tomb. The exhumation, which attracted worldwide media attention, rekindled the debate about Franco's legacies in present-day Spain. For some on the Right, moving Franco's corpse was not only a scandalous affront to the dictator and his family, but unnecessary to boot. Spain, they argued, had fully settled its accounts with its conflictive past decades ago, when, shortly after Franco's death, it became a full-fledged democracy. For others, the exhumation was the proper way to consummate the final break between democratic Spain and the dictatorship: the belated but much-needed last touch on a forty-five-year process of democratic transition. For yet others, it was a mere symbolic gesture that only confirmed how much remains to be done for Spain to truly come to terms with the legacies of its three-year civil war (1936–39) and thirty-six years of institutionalized state violence (1939–75).

For a former dictator, Franco enjoys an unusually revered status in democratic Spain. Unlike other twentieth-century tyrants, he died in bed, on November 20, 1975, almost forty years after his involvement, as a young military officer, in an attempted coup d'état that would unleash a bloody three-year civil war. That war was won by the self-identified "Nationalists," under Franco's leadership, with significant backing from Nazi Germany and Fascist Italy. Franco was head of state from 1939 until his death. Starting in the 1950s, he enjoyed the support of the United States; in late 1955, Spain was admitted to the United Nations.

Small in stature and endowed with an unusually high-pitched voice, Franco ruled his country with an iron hand. Hundreds of thousands of Spaniards were forced into exile; tens of thousands of supporters of the Republic were executed, imprisoned, or interned in concentration camps. Public expressions of Catalan, Basque, and Galician language and culture were proscribed in the name of national unity, along with anything else that did not jibe with Franco's image of Spanish identity and history, in which Catholicism and empire figured prominently. The public sphere was heavily censored. "Spain has seven enemies," one of the lessons in an official elementary-school textbook read: "liberalism, democracy, Judaism, Freemasonry, Marxism, capitalism, and separatism." Despite Franco's avowed distaste for capitalism, in the 1950s and '60s his regime modernized Spain's economy, as industrialization and mass tourism pushed economic growth to record levels.

Once the old dictator was dead, Spain quickly became a democracy in a relatively peaceful—but by no means bloodless—transition that was long held up as an international model. The Franco regime and the democratic opposition were able to reach a compromise: political parties were legalized—even the Communists were allowed back in—while all politically motivated crimes committed in the preceding thirty-nine years were forgiven in a general amnesty. This meant not only that thousands of the regime's political prisoners went free—a key priority for the opposition at the time—but also that every representative of the government, regardless of rank or rap sheet, got to start over with a clean slate.

In the absence of any kind of purge or accountability, existing power structures remained largely intact. Everyone could stay put, whether they were politicians, judges, mayors, television producers, chiefs of police, state functionaries, or university professors. The families, banks, and corporations that had thrived under the regime, accumulating power, prestige, and wealth, were allowed to keep their capital, land, and nobility titles. Even Franco's hand-picked successor, the thirty-seven-year-old Juan Carlos de Borbón, who was crowned days after the dictator's death, simply remained on the throne.

The fact that the Amnesty Law would later bar the thousands of victims of the dictatorship from seeking justice was not on many Spaniards' minds at the time. The majority of the population agreed with the political leadership that it was more important to look toward the future than to wallow in the past. For many, the fear of a new civil war—and the desire to avoid that scenario at all costs—was also front and center. The predominant sensations were relief or pride, if not indifference.

Yet over the past twenty years or so, a growing number of Spaniards have seen these feelings of relief, pride, and indifference turn into indignation. The Spanish transition began to look decidedly less exemplary in the 1990s, as countries like Chile, Argentina, and South Africa showed it was possible to process a violent past in different ways, through truth commissions—or even trials in which former military and political leaders ended up convicted. "Why has impunity reigned in our country?" younger generations began to wonder; "why haven't we been able to come to terms with Francoism?"

After years of neglect, the thousands of unmarked mass graves from the civil war that continued to litter the country drew the attention of media and civil society as teams of volunteers engaged in improvised exhumation projects. Around the same time, younger progressives began to understand the country's chronic problems, including political corruption and economic inequality, as symptoms of the improperly processed past. This trend intensified in the wake of the Great Recession. The *indignados* who, in the spring and summer of 2011, occupied public urban spaces for months on end and later organized themselves politically in parties like Podemos, waved the flag of the Second Republic (1931–39) and denounced what they now, disparagingly, called the "regime of 1978." "They call it a democracy," they chanted, "but that's not what it is!"

In 2007, under the previous socialist government, the Spanish parliament adopted a law that included a set of cautious first steps to settle some of the accounts left unattended in 1978. The annual gathering to honor Franco at the Valley of Fallen, for example, was finally declared illegal, while state subsidies were made available for families who sought to exhume their loved ones from a mass grave. Still, for many critics the law was woefully insufficient. While attempts to bring judicial charges against regime officials ran up against the Amnesty Law, international pressure increased. In 2015, the United Nations' human rights commission concluded that the Amnesty Law should be rescinded because it had become a serious impediment for investigations into human rights violations (Faber 2018, 86–87). UN spokespeople also noted that the Spanish government was failing to meet its obligations toward the many victims of torture and forced disappearance. To remedy these deficits, the UN has urged Spain to institute a truth commission.

So far, however, the government in Madrid has preferred to sidestep such recommendations. After all, the potential presence of Francoist legacies in Spain today is a politically sensitive matter. The escalation around Catalonia's bid for independence has only served to increase the discomfort, as Spain's handling of the Catalan crisis has sown doubts about the functioning of its rule of law and respect for constitutional liberties. Similar doubts had already emerged in 2015 when the government of Prime Minister Mariano Rajoy passed a controversial "gag law" that, among other things, brandished the notion of "citizen safety" to limit the legal right to protest and impose hefty fines on journalists covering police malfeasance. According to the *New York Times* editorial board, the law "disturbingly harken[ed] back to the dark days of the Franco regime."

The years following proved that the critics had been right to worry. Spanish citizens have been slapped with steep fines for protesting without permission, criticizing police, blocking an eviction, or offending the King. In 2017, a young woman was convicted to a year in prison for "extolling terrorism" after she'd tweeted an old joke about Luis Carrero Blanco, Franco's second-in-command, who had been killed in a spectacular operation by ETA, in 1973— that is, during the dictatorship. (The Supreme Court later exonerated her.) In early October 2019, it was revealed that a woman who, the year before, had joined the activists of Femen in a topless protest against a neofascist tribute to Franco, and who'd been beaten and kicked by the neofascists, was fined 300 euros for "disturbing public safety" with "a nude upper body" and "slogans against the meeting." As it happened, the tribute to Franco had been approved by the authorities, while Femen's protest had not (Borraz 2019). In a similarly curious asymmetry, the Franco Foundation, which seeks to promote the dictator's legacy, is perfectly legal in Spain, receiving subsidies from the state into the twenty-first century. To be sure, the Spanish legal code follows European trends in that it prohibits publicly extolling any group found guilty of genocide or crimes against humanity. The problem is that Francoism was never put on trial. (In late October 2018, the European Parliament passed a motion against the rise of neofascist violence in Europe that included several incidents in Spain. Among other things, the motion condemned the Franco Foundation as "an entity that glorifies a dictatorship and its crimes.")

The regional "separatists" are not the only ones who believe that Franco's ghost still wields power over Spain. In November 2019, one of the Catalan independence movement's staunchest critics, the journalist Antonio Maestre, published *Franquismo, S.A.* (Francoism, Inc.), a book that reveals the extent to which the roots of today's corporate and political corruption can be found in the close ties that the Franco regime established with the businessmen and bankers who supported the Nationalist coup. A sizeable part of Spain's largest corporations and wealthiest families today, Maestre writes, "owe their prominent positions to their collaboration with the regime." The benefits they received in exchange for their support ranged from nobility titles and profitable monopolies to the use of cheap labor from (political) prisoners. For these corporations and families—which included Catalans and Basques—the democratic transition was a mere blip on the screen: they were allowed "to continue to function normally." Maestre draws a comparison with Germany, where companies that collaborated with the Nazi regime or profited from prison labor were eventually forced to pay reparations. In Spain, such a measure seems still far off. (See Chapter 11 for an interview with Maestre.)

Emilio Silva, too, believes that there is an endless laundry list of issues from the Civil War and the Franco period that are yet to be settled. "Franco's body symbolizes an enormous democratic deficit," Silva wrote in a column in late September 2019. Among the institutions that most benefited from the regime but have never been held accountable for it is the Catholic Church. The Spanish judiciary, too, is a relatively closed guild in which reactionaries find a comfortable home. Silva expressed skepticism about the significance of the dictator's exhumation. For one, he pointed out, Franco's new resting place is still a public cemetery, maintained, just like the Valley of the Fallen, by the taxpayers. "That's a slap in the face of the regime's victims," he told me. "How can you make them to pay for his tomb?" In that sense, it would have been more fitting if, in October 2019, Franco's mummy had slipped from its coffin and crashed to the ground; his victims, too, have had their bones and skulls exposed every time a mass grave is dug up. (See Chapter 16 for an interview with Silva.)

Now that the dictator's tomb is empty, what will happen to the Valley? Whether it will become a "memorial for the fight against fascism," as Prime Minister Sánchez suggested in 2018, remains to be seen. The idea to re-invent the Valley is not new; something similar had been suggested in 2011 by a blue-ribbon commission appointed by the previous Socialist government—although its report was then ignored through the seven years of conservative rule that followed it. "That Franco had to leave was obvious," Francisco Ferrándiz, a social anthropologist who specializes in exhumations and who was a member of the commission, told me in October 2019. "But it's not clear what possibilities for change the Valley offers. In 2011, I personally believed it could still be turned into a site of reconciliation. By now, I've changed my mind. The monument's entire design is the expression of a totalitarian worldview. One option that might be feasible is to turn it into an educational space, following the example of the Nazi concentration camps." (Some of the recommendations from 2011 were incorporated into the new Law of Democratic Memory proposed in September 2020.)

One of Ferrándiz's fellow members on the commission, the Catalan historian Ricard Vinyes, believes that any attempt to turn the Valley into something else is futile—in part because the monument is in such bad shape. "The monument was born sickly. Today, it's a dying body," he wrote in a newspaper column in December 2019. To prevent its collapse, due in large part to ongoing water damage, would cost "extravagant" amounts of money. "Worse, such an investment will only postpone, not stop, its transformation into a ruin." The question at hand, he wrote, "is not how to save the monument with pedagogical fantasies . . . that don't transcend the museum," but "how to accompany the ruin," so that any visitor may "look and think, choose, interpellate, and perhaps construct an image or a decision about the past." To be sure, schools should teach about the Valley, its history and its purpose. But the monument itself should exhibit "its ethical, political, and religious collapse" (Vinyes 2019). (See Chapter 15 for an interview with Vinyes.)

The Francoist monument is not the only structure in danger of collapse, the journalist Guillem Martínez warned in late September 2019. For all its progressive symbolism, he wrote, Franco's exhumation was a distraction from the fact that Spain's rule of law is rapidly eroding. "The state has taken an authoritarian turn," Martínez argued. He was referring not only to the 2015 gag law but also to the changed role of the monarchy—which in 2017 adopted an unusually politicized stance toward Catalonia—and the way the judicialization of the Catalan conflict has served as an excuse for the authorities to undermine the right to protest under the banner of "security" or "national unity." "Concepts like democracy, rebellion, sedition or terrorism only function if they are crystal clear," Martínez wrote. "Instead, they are becoming more elastic by the day." (See Chapter 4 for an interview with Martínez.)

The November 2019 elections provided an opportunity for all parties to use the controversy over Franco to their electoral advantage. While the Partido Popular (PP) accused Prime Minister Sánchez of opportunism, it did not hesitate for throw oil on the fire and resuscitate the specter of civil war. "Instead of working toward the unity of all Spaniards, Sánchez is trying to divide us. Because that's the roadmap of the Left," Isabel Díaz Ayuso, the PP's president of the Madrid region, said in early October. "The targets of his attacks are clear: the Transition, the monarchy, the flag, and the Constitution." The Socialists are homing in on Franco now, she said. What will be next? "The cross at the Valley of the Fallen? The entire Valley? Or will churches burn again, as they did in 1936?" (Caballero 2019). The debates preceding Sánchez's investiture at the helm of a progressive coalition government in early January 2020 continued in the same vein, with several leaders quoting Manuel Azaña, Spain's president in the years of the Second Republic (Pardo Torregrosa 2020). Javier Ortega Smith, a deputy for Vox, spent part of the debate ostentatiously reading from a recent book by Stanley Payne, a conservative US historian, entitled *In Defense of Spain*. "The Communists Who Provoked the Civil War Return to Government," the right-wing media outlet *Intereconomía* tweeted in early January 2020.

Meanwhile, public opinion polls conducted around Franco's exhumation confirmed that Spaniards were seriously divided—not only on the desirability of removing the dictator from his tomb but on the very nature of his regime. According to a poll by the newspaper *ElDiario.es*, almost three quarters of PP voters believed Franco's body should have been left alone (Cortizo 2019). A poll by the television network LaSexta went one step further: some 37 percent of the PP base did not think that Franco had been a dictator. Among Vox voters, that percentage rose to 58 percent (2019).

That ideology would color citizens' view of the past is perhaps no surprise. But these polls also have a practical explanation. History education in Spain leaves much to be desired, says Fernando Hernández Sánchez, who trains secondary school teachers at the Autonomous University of Madrid. Every year, he asks his first-year students what they were taught in school about twentieth-century Spain. Most of them know who Franco was, to be sure. But beyond that many are at a loss. Their lack of preparation is symptomatic, Hernández says. In a national poll from 2010, a third of respondents agreed with the statement that, compared with the present, there was more "order and peace" during the Franco years. Almost 70 percent said they had been taught little to nothing about the Spanish Civil War. Forty percent said that both "sides" carried equal blame, and more than a third believed each side had caused the same number of victims. (The historian Paul Preston concluded in 2012 that "repression by the rebels was about three times greater than that which took place in the Republican zone" [xvii–xviii]). Close to sixty percent stated that "Franco-ism had both good and bad things." More than half did not know when the Constitution was approved (Hernández Sánchez 2014, 185). Although no comparable poll has been conducted in the past ten years, Hernández told me in late 2019 that the situation has not improved: "To the contrary. Our knowledge of the past is a black hole that is only growing. And this situation is generating serious political consequences."

The simplified narrative that long upheld the legitimacy of the Spanish transition to democracy is losing credibility, Hernández said. "We shouldn't forget that, going by the population statistics of 2017, 43 percent of Spain's more than forty-six million inhabitants were born after the adoption of the 1978 Constitution, while more than 40 percent of those who are now adults did not have a chance to vote on it." In this context, Hernández says, it is urgent to create space for the emergence of a new historical narrative about the origins of Spain's current democracy. "The reality of the Transition was much more complex, unstable, indeterminate, dramatic, and open-ended than the canonical story suggests. The new generations of Spaniards deserve a truthful account, not a fairy tale." What such a story would look like is clear: "The freedoms we now enjoy were not simply gifted to us. Nor did they materialize based on a symbolic handshake between leaders. No, those freedoms were conquered with hard sacrifices. They were paid for in blood and suffering." To make it possible to tell this story, however, it is necessary to adjust some of the central premises of the standard version of events, Hernández points out—including the premise that has been celebrated as the Transition's most shining achievement: "the idea that, for the first time in our modern history, we Spaniards managed not to kill each other." This premise is false. In fact, "by the 1970s, the likelihood of a new civil war was non-existent."

Spanish students today learn about twentieth- and twenty-first century history in the equivalent of tenth grade, where they are expected to cover more than four centuries of world history in a year's time. For those who continue beyond the obligatory education, they do this once again in the eleventh grade, in preparation for the college entrance exam. "The history curriculum for fifteen and sixteen year olds is heavily overloaded," David Fernández de Arriba, a thirty-four-year-old high school history teacher from Catalonia, told me in the fall of 2019 (Faber 2019b). "We only teach three hours of history per week. And we start in the seventeenth century. This means that the Spanish Civil War doesn't come up until the very end of the year—if we don't run out of time, that is. Getting to cover the Franco period is even less likely. Just the other day I was talking to my colleagues at the school where I teach. Many said they, as students, had never gotten around to the Civil War at all. Of course, for some teachers and schools it's a convenient excuse to avoid a still controversial topic."

"There clearly exists a political will to keep things the way they are," Fernández added. "Otherwise, the situation would have been addressed through a curricular reform a long time ago." In addition to the unfortunate timing, the textbooks themselves leave much to be desired, he said. "They tend to treat the war and the dictatorship in ways that are extremely superficial. Often, they also adopt the notion that 'both sides' carry blame, since 'atrocities were committed by both.'" As scholars like Paloma Aguilar and Pablo Sánchez León have argued, this view of the Civil War is in effect a legacy of late Francoism.

For Hernández, too, the key to opening this space for a

new collective narrative is secondary-school education, in particular the history classroom. An uninformed public has proven to be fertile ground for right-wing myths. "Unless we change the paradigm, there will never be enough time to teach our most recent history," Hernández told me. "No student should graduate without an understanding of the processes that have shaped the society they are about to enter as a subject with full political rights," he said. "This is why the twentieth century deserves its own entire year, covering Spanish history from the turn of the century through the 1980s." Redesigning the curriculum in this way "won't yield immediate results," he admitted, "nor will it be a miracle cure against reactionary populism and its political effects." But, he added, "at least it will help avoid a scenario in which, in a not-too-far-away future, we'll look back on the Middle Ages as period of relative progress."

FURTHER READING

Although it was published over a decade ago, Tremlett's *Ghosts of Spain* (2007) continues to be an insightful and highly readable English-language introduction to the achievements and contradictions of the first thirty years of post-Franco democracy. Franco's biography is masterfully narrated by Preston (1994), whose more recent book on the history of political corruption and incompetence in Spain (2020) is also a great read. Good English-language histories of the Civil War and the subsequent Francoist repression include Richards (1998, 2013) and Graham (2005, 2012). For recent accounts of the Second Republic, the Civil War, and

Francoism that question the dominant progressive narratives from a liberal-conservative point of view, see Payne (2019), Ruiz (2015), and Seidman (2011). For more on the exhumations and their significance in a comparative perspective, see Ferrándiz (2014), in Spanish, and Ferrándiz and Robben (2015), in English.

2

Surreptitious Survival

My first encounter with unadulterated Francoism took place in the fall of 1992, in the third month of my year of study abroad in Spain. The morning of Sunday, November 22, found me among an upbeat crowd at the capital's Plaza de Oriente, in view of the Royal Palace. "It's busy," I wrote in a piece for a Dutch magazine that came out soon after. "There are vendors selling flags, hats, and pins; others peddle posters and calendars. I see couples, both young and elderly, groups of teenage boys and girls enjoying themselves: a cross-section of the population. Then, suddenly, music starts playing from loudspeakers. As if obeying an inaudible order, right arms are raised everywhere. The bright red-and-yellow bands affixed above the elbows catch the sunlight. And about eight thousand throats bellow the words to 'Cara al sol,' the anthem of the Falange" (Faber 1993, 34).

What I'd witnessed, it turned out, was the annual commemoration of the anniversary of Franco's death. In 1992 Franco would have turned one hundred; but the special anniversary found Spain's Far Right divided. "Fewer than

8,000 people attended the event, according to police estimates," the newspaper *El País* reported the next day, noting
it as one of the lowest attendance records in seventeen years.
(The organizers claimed there were seventy-five thousand
people present.) "Unlike previous manifestations of the Far
Right, the dearth of paramilitary uniforms and Nazi symbols was noticeable," the reporter wrote. Yet compared to
previous years there were more calls against immigration
and for "a Christian Europe." Among the speakers was Antonio María Oriol, former Minister of Justice under Franco,
who called for the defense "of the grand ideals of God and
Spain" (Mercado 1992).

Twenty-eight years later, flag-waving groups of Spanish
citizens with their right arm stretched out singing Francoist
hymns are still a recurring feature of the urban landscape. In
fact, as I am writing this, in January 2020, my Twitter feed
is showing protests across Spain "for Spanish unity" and
against the progressive government, a coalition between Pedro Sánchez's social-democratic PSOE and Pablo Iglesias's
Unidas Podemos, which was voted in with support from
Basque and Catalan parties who favor independence for
their regions. In Barcelona, protestors gathered before the
city hall are brandishing Francoist flags, bringing the same
salutes, and singing the same hymns that I heard in 1992.
In addition to praising Franco, today they are cursing Barcelona's city government, headed by former anti-eviction
activist Ada Colau. "Long live Spain," they shout, while
hurling ethnic slurs and sexually derogatory terms at the
city's first woman mayor, who is bisexual.

"Spain is two thousand years old, it's mentioned in the
Bible," said a Vox protestor in Madrid who was interviewed

on television later that evening. Another protestor claimed the new government—voted in with a parliamentary plurality following general elections—had perpetrated nothing less than a coup d'état. Asked about Franco's ascent to power, he said: "Franco did not commit a coup. What he did was saving Spain." Yet another protestor assured the interviewer that the left-wing "coup" was bankrolled by George Soros and the Freemasons (LaSexta 2020).

Shocking though they may be to an outside observer, these conspicuous manifestations of Francoist ideas and behavior are not the only traces of the dictatorship remaining in Spain today. Nor are they the most important. More useful for understanding the surreptitious survival of Francoist ways of thinking and operating is a concept popularized by the author Manuel Vázquez Montalbán: *el franquismo socio-lógico*, a term he used to signify the long-lasting, collective aftereffects—in physical, political, and psychological terms—of close to forty years' worth of a one-party system, censorship, reactionary nationalism, religious zeal, persecution of political dissidence, widespread corruption, and a culture of surveillance in which citizens were encouraged to inform on each other (Moret 1992; Vázquez Montalbán 1992). The term's weakness for analytical purposes is its lack of definition, the historian Pablo Sánchez León pointed out when I interviewed him in January 2020. Still, he added, it can be most useful when it's invoked not to refer to "a particular social group," or even a collective identity. Rather, what the concept points to is "a particular social psychology, a series of habits and practices that describe a large segment of the population of post-Franco Spain." Along these lines, Vázquez Montalbán's term has been deployed over the past couple of decades to describe a wide range of legacies of the Franco regime that have outlasted the dictator's death. Here is a tentative inventory.

Francoism has survived most obviously in institutional structures, beginning with the figure of the head of state. Spain became a republic in 1931; Franco declared victory eight years later. As noted, it was the dictator himself who, in 1969, laid the basis for a restoration of the monarchy when he had Juan Carlos, the grandson of the country's last king, named as his successor. But while it's true that Spaniards overwhelmingly voted in favor of the 1978 Constitution, which defined Spain as a parliamentary monarchy, they were never given the opportunity to indicate whether they preferred a return to a republican form of government. It was Adolfo Suárez, prime minister when the Transition was brokered, who single-handedly decided to maintain the monarchy, as he confessed in a 1995 interview with the journalist Victoria Prego that was kept from the public for years (LaSexta 2016b). While designing the Law for Political Reform, which was approved by Franco's parliament in 1976 and laid the basis for the Transition, Suárez slipped in the monarchy as a package deal, he recalled in the interview, which was recorded on camera. He then covered his lapel mic, indicating that what followed would be off the record, and said, almost chuckling: "It was simple: the majority of foreign government leaders requested that I hold a referendum about [the choice between] monarchy or republic. . . . [But] I had polls conducted, [which indicated that] we'd lose. So, at that point I included the words 'king' and 'monarchy' in the law, and told them they'd already been submitted to a referendum."

Although the monarchy is Franco's most visible post-humous gift to Spain, other central state institutions still look a lot like their Francoist predecessors as well. The Audiencia Nacional, the national criminal court in Madrid, for example, is the direct continuation of Franco's Court of Public Order (Tribunal de Orden Público). Today, the court has jurisdiction over the entire national territory; it specializes in "major crimes," including crimes against the monarchy, terrorism, financial crimes, drug trafficking, and international crimes. In the years following the Transition, it was the Audiencia Nacional that took on the prosecution of ETA, the armed wing of the Basque independence movement that committed acts of terrorism—in part because the courts in Basque country itself were thought to be subject to undue pressure. It was at the same court from which, in the 1990s and early 2000s, Judge Baltasar Garzón, invoking universal jurisdiction, prosecuted former heads of state in Latin America and elsewhere for human rights violations. Following Catalonia's failed bid for independence in 2017, it was the Audiencia Nacional, rather than a Catalan court, that first prosecuted the politicians and activists accused of "rebellion" and "sedition." As we'll see in Chapter 5, this type of court is an exception in Europe and presents serious juridical problems. Yet what many see as a more urgent problem affecting the judiciary is its staunch conservatism, which is often explained through the fact that the judiciary was not purged, reformed, or renewed following the transition to democracy.

If the courts have allowed some elements of Francoism to survive, central parts of the legal code, too, have taken long to reform. Divorce wasn't legalized until 1981; laws targeting the LGBTQ community stayed on the books until 1989. (To make things worse, people convicted under those laws were excluded from the 1977 amnesty.) Critics have also lamented the fact that the judiciary has consistently upheld Francoist jurisprudence—including thousands of convictions by military tribunals of individuals accused of "rebellion" for their defense of the democratically elected Republican government against the military coup of 1936. What has driven this legal conservatism is not just a concern with juridical integrity, Carlos Jiménez Villarejo and Antonio Doñate Martín wrote in a 2012 book on the topic, but ideology pure and simple. The Francoist judges and prosecutors who kept their positions through the Transition, the historian Josep Fontana writes in the prologue, not only sought to "erase the memory of the crimes of Francoism," but became the self-appointed custodians of Francoist values (2012). Residing at the heart of Spain's judicial branch, the authors write in the introduction, is "a certain Francoist ideological bias, authoritarian in character, which is the direct result of a Transition that barely affected the judiciary, which meant that the judiciary accepted the values of democracy only very slowly" (2012).

As Antonio Maestre explains in an interview in Chapter 11 of this book, one of the most powerful continuities from dictatorship to democracy has been economic in nature. "In the Spanish economy, it's very difficult to find entrepreneurs or self-made men or women who did not get started or consolidate their enterprises during Francoism," he writes in a recent book on the topic. "In 1979, the magazine *Fomento de la Producción* published a list of the 100 richest persons [in Spain] at that moment. Those names of people who amassed their fortunes during Francoism are still on the lists of the richest and most powerful today" (Maestre 2019a, chapters 3 and 13) On the other hand, as the journalist Miguel Mora pointed out, although many large corporations are linked to Francoist families, "many have by now been sold to global investment funds, even if the family names survive in the board room." And while corporate capital accumulated under Franco holds a firm grip on the mainstream media, globalization has shaken things up in that sector as well, the journalist Miquel Ramos told me. "The media landscape is increasingly international, controlled by large multinational conglomerates," he said.

Two other important channels of institutional continuity are the Catholic Church and the university system. Although democratic Spain is formally founded on a separation of church and state, the Catholic hierarchy has for years enjoyed special treatment from the authorities that is not granted to any other organized religion—especially in the area of education. "Spain's agreements with the Vatican have barely been touched since the Franco years," the editor Magda Bandera told me, "although it looks like that may finally be about to change. Still, the Catholic Church has deeply penetrated the public education system, and Spain has an unusually high number of semi-private hospitals that are governed by religious orders." National holidays, too, are overwhelmingly religious. They moreover reflect a decidedly Francoist view of Spanish history, Ramos said. "We still celebrate as heroic feats what were often episodes of genocide. The colonization of the Americas, for example, or the conquest of Granada and the expulsion of the Muslims."

"The university administrations and faculty that collaborated with the regime for forty years were largely left alone during the Transition," the historian Luis de Guezala told me. "There were no major changes, let alone purges of any kind." This continuity contrasts sharply with the ruthless purge that the dictatorship imposed on Spain's academic landscape in the years immediately following the civil war. "As far as the university was concerned, the impact of the war can be compared to that of an atomic bomb," Miguel de Lucas wrote recently. "The initial destruction was intensified by several decades' worth of radiation. Some classrooms are still not free of contamination" (2017). The corruption scandals that have shaken the academic community in recent years are clear symptoms, he told me.

"Many of the worst dynamics of institutional inbreeding and servility that we see in Spanish universities today began before the Francoist period," the anthropologist Francisco Ferrándiz told me. "Still, they were reinforced in the years of the dictatorship and the institutional resistance to change is very strong. Despite important improvements, the sediment is still active in our day-to-day practice. Sadly, younger generations of faculty have been assimilated into it and have accepted it as natural in their doctoral apprenticeships and the struggle for positions."

The contemporary Spanish university descends more directly from Francoism than from the Second Republic, the Catalan historian Jaume Claret argued in a groundbreaking study of the Francoist repression of academic life (Claret Miranda 2006). "In recent years, Spanish universities have finally begun coming to terms with this part of their own histories," he told me in an interview. "They have also begun to commemorate the victims of Francoist repression among their ranks." Yet much remains to be done, he added. "For one, we still don't have an 'inclusive' Spanish history that takes into account the contributions of the thousands of scholars and writers who were forced into exile, but whose careers were often initiated here in Spain. Similarly, many scholars, especially women, are not or insufficiently credited for their contributions and discoveries. And some disciplines still have not properly revised their own institutional history—including the ways the regime instrumentalized them for its purposes."

Another glaring holdover from the Francoist period is the lack of transparency of the Spanish democratic state, which is reflected most visibly in the Law of Official Secrets. Adopted in 1968, this legislation continues to shield whole swaths of government documents from public scrutiny. Despite persistent protests from researchers and civil society, successive governments of the democratic period have been unable or unwilling to revise this law. "Nobody seems to know" how many secrets it protects from declassification, Jesús Rodríguez wrote in *El País* in December 2019. "Maybe they prefer not to know," he added. "According to different sources, the issues that Spain holds under lock and key include controversial episodes from the Francoist repression; the decolonization of Morocco, the Ifni, and Equatorial Guinea; . . . [and] the preparation and development of the failed 1981 military coup." According to Henar Alonso, an administrator at the General Military Archive in Ávila interviewed by Rodríguez, the current situation is the direct legacy of "a secretive paranoia generated by a dictatorship blocked in by a civil war, a world war, and a cold war" (Rodríguez 2019). Remnants of this paranoia clearly survive in the modus operandi of the Spanish state today.

Received ideas and narratives are another broad area in which Francoist legacies thrive. The notion, for instance, that Franco imposed "peace and order"—as Franco himself liked to phrase it—on an incurably unruly nation continues to loom large in Spanish public opinion. "Dictatorships don't have freedom, but they do have a certain peace and order because everyone knows what to expect," the liberal political leader Albert Rivera told a journalist after he returned from a trip to Venezuela, suggesting that Maduro's Venezuela was worse off than Spain had been under Franco (ElDiario 2016). (Rivera's dismissive comments also illustrated the extent to which current politicians' views of Latin America are indebted to Franco's policy of *Hispanidad*, which imagined the Spanish-speaking world paternalistically as a tight-knit family united by language and religion, in which Spain continued to fulfill a guiding role [Faber 2008].) The positive memory of the dictatorship can be confusing to outsiders, the journalist and literary scholar Miguel de Lucas told me. "I teach Spanish history to American students who are spending a semester in Seville," he said. "Their family stays are overwhelmingly in the richest, oldest area of the city. More than once, students will come up to me and say: 'I'm confused. Was Franco a good or bad guy? You've taught us he did bad things, but my guest mother tells me he wasn't so bad at all.'"

If Francoism is associated with peace and order, democracy, by contrast, is often correlated with conflict, which in turn is seen in a negative light. This semantic map, too, was a central element of Franco's legitimation of, first, his coup and, second, his decades-long, nondemocratic rule. As Elena Delgado (2014) and Ricard Vinyes (2009) have argued, Spain's young democracy has been profoundly marked by the idea that conflict is something to be avoided at all costs. Politicians' constant invocation of a "democratic normality" associated with "low levels of tension or the resolution of conflicts through a constant appeal to forms of consensus that exclude 'ideology,'" Delgado writes, has "instituted the common sense of Spanish democracy." This common sense has also fetishized the notion of unity, based on the idea that any kind of social or political fracture along ideological, regional, or linguistic lines "endangers the very existence of the nation" (2014, 32).

Francoist habits die hard in other areas as well. Common phrases, tropes, and frames to describe the twentieth-century past and the current political landscape often hark back to official Francoist discourse. It's still common for politicians and voters on the right to label anyone on the left disparagingly as *rojo*, or "red," for example, or to refer to citizens who would like to see their regions become independent from Spain as *separatistas* or agents of *la anti-España*. Similarly, when speaking about the Civil War, textbooks and politicians regularly identify both the Nationalists and the Republicans as *bandos*, or "sides"—a term that, by suggesting the equivalency of a sporting match, glosses over the fact that the war started when the Nationalists perpetrated a coup against a democratically elected government. And if Francoist symbols, street names, and statues continue to be legion in public spaces throughout the country—despite the 2007 law calling for their removal—legacies of the dictatorship have proven persistent in cultural life as well. As Fernando Larraz (2009) has shown, for example, the master narrative of Spanish literary historiography is still largely shaped by the templates established during the Franco years. Worse, many literary texts that were first published in those years are still reprinted in their censored versions (Larraz 2014).

And yet the prodigious presence of Francoist fossils in Spain today does not necessarily say much about their relative weight or importance in the country's day-to-day existence. How significant a force is sociological Francoism in Spanish society and institutions? Between late 2019 and early 2020 I asked some twenty-five Spanish writers, scholars, and journalists what they thought. Predictably, opinions differed.

"If we take sociological Francoism to signify the adherence to the institutions of the Francoist state," said Noelia Adánez, a writer and political commentator, "then I do not think it is a significant force any longer. It's true, of course, that the vision of the state prevailing in the judiciary can be seen as a holdover from the past. The same, for that matter, is true of the disproportionate influence of the Catholic Church on educational policies. But I would say that these features, by now, more than forty years after the Transition, have less to do with sociological Francoism per se than with the way Spain has decided to shape its democracy. Even when a party like Vox, whose extreme positions extend to other parties on the Right as well, seems to deploy a Francoist imaginary, we should not be fooled. In the end, Spain's Far Right today is much more in tune with the Far Right elsewhere in Europe than with the Francoist past."

Jordi Gracia, an academic and public intellectual, agreed

that the Spanish Far Right is less Francoist than aligned with global developments. What Vox has done, he told me, is to politically resurrect the "moral, ideological, and even picturesque ingredients of the most rancid Right." To be sure, these may include a vague nostalgia for the Francoist years and its touchstones. Yet, he said, "I don't see a consistent defense of the dictatorship as such." In his view, the voters who feel an attraction for the Far Right are "the bewildered children of globalization" who feel threatened by "the political power of the Left, and surely, too, by the combined effect of two unexpected waves: the demands of feminism and the growth of the Catalan independence movement."

Montse Armengou, a documentary filmmaker and television producer at the Catalan public television network, sees things differently. "To me, it's crystal clear that sociological Francoism today is alive and well," she told me. "Its manifestations are manifold. In the judiciary, it's not only expressed in the shameful lack of reparations for the victims of the regime but also, for example, in the way that courts have dealt with the Catalan crisis, or in their outrageous treatment of women who are victims of sexual violence." For Armengou, the continued power of Francoist ideas to influence Spain's political and social present rests on two pillars. "The first of these pillars is the refusal to establish a clean break with the regime, condemning it both ethically and judicially, and to initiate reparations for the damage it did. The second pillar is the fact that many of those in power are biological, sociological, and economic heirs of the Francoist elites. To this day, they continue to exercise that power, whether it's in politics, the economy, or the media. Mind you," she added, "these heirs may be perfect democrats, so to so speak. I am not saying they are fascists. But they are determined to hold on to their power. And they will reject any measure that they believe will threaten their privilege—even if this means simply condemning the Franco regime."

Armengou's position is shared by Cristina Fallarás, a writer, journalist, and editor. "Almost everything in Spain today is Francoist or a legacy of Francoism," she told me, pointing to the ideology of the Spanish Right, political corruption, and the lack of justice for victims of the dictatorship. "The Catholic Church, which was the main pillar on which the regime rested, is still all-powerful in this country—and still profoundly Francoist," she said. The Valencian novelist Alfons Cervera is on the same page. "This democracy simply has not been capable of building its own democratic culture," he told me. "If you'll allow me to use an old-fashioned term, I'd say that the *values* that hold sway in many spheres of society are still the values we've inherited from the Francoist period."

Ángel Viñas, a retired diplomat and prominent historian of the Civil War, agrees with Armengou and Cervera about the persistence of Francoist habits and reflexes in present-day Spain. Yet for him, that persistence is less a source of concern than an historical inevitability: "It's impossible from one day to the next to eradicate something that was instituted during forty long years of dictatorship, whether we are talking about society, the economy, institutions, or mentalities," he said. "While many state structures slowly adapted to the reforms of the Transition, the resistance to change was significant." The continued presence of groups

such as ETA, the militant Basque pro-independence organization that perpetrated terrorist attacks until 2011, put a
significant brake on democratic renewal, whether in ideological or institutional terms, Viñas added. "Still, Spain is
much less of an exception in Western Europe than many
Spaniards tend to assume," he argued. "Take Germany. The
de-Nazification that the Allies initiated in what would soon
become West Germany was really quite superficial. Ade-
nauer preferred to quickly establish a democratic regime
over a large-scale 'purification' of the country. Add to that
the Cold War, which needed a strong West Germany, and
the fact that many of the state employees, army officials,
police officers, and judges who were necessary to build that
new regime had been, or continued to be, Nazis. It took until the early 1960s for things in Germany to change, and even
then they did so slowly." Other European countries have
similar profiles, Viñas pointed out. "Italy, France, or Bel-
gium also did not significantly change the social or material
bases of the regimes that ruled them during World War II."

For the historian Carles Sirera, the role of the European Union is also more complicated than critics of the
Transition have made it seem. The dominant ideas in Spain
about European "normality" or "democracy," he told me,
"don't allow us to properly assess the survival of Francoist
elites in Spain. The truth is, however, that the upper echelons of the state, including the Supreme Court and the foreign service, are still largely controlled by Madrid-based
families united by their collaboration with the Franco regime." These families, he added, still today constitute a tight
social network marked by an "authoritarian" outlook and a
"closed mentality." This network extends into the business

world, although, he adds, "the private sector has been less closed to talent and is therefore socially less homogeneous."

For Sirera, the constitution of this power bloc goes back much further than the 1936 coup. "Its origins lie, first, in the moderate, more authoritarian strains of nineteenth-century liberalism and, second, in Spanish neo-Catholicism. Starting in the mid-nineteenth century, both have aimed to create a hierarchical society united by Catholic and national values, a society capable of joining economic modernity without suffering the disintegrating effects associated with the free market, such as materialism and secularization." Spain is not unique in this regard, Sirera points out; similar currents have existed in other non-Protestant European countries. Still, two features set Spain apart: "a marked imperial nostalgia, rooted in the fact that Spain was a world power before the rise of the Protestant capitalist nations," and the fact that Franco won the Spanish Civil War. Franco's victory, Sirera told me, meant that Spain's master narrative would diverge from that of much of the rest of Western Europe after World War II. France and Italy built their postwar democracies on a progressive, antifascist consensus. In post-Francoist Spain, by contrast, "fascism and Communism were construed as comparable evils, so that a commitment to democracy was reduced to an instrumental agreement whose main goal was to maintain peace and order." In this framework, fascism was little more than "a minor evil," albeit one cloaked in the prestige of having won the war.

Elitist, antidemocratic forms of liberalism exist through-out Europe, Sirera said. "But what sets Spain apart is that here, this current of thought is the glue that holds the elites together. In the rest of Europe, the collaborationist positions of the antidemocratic elites during World War II made them the object of reproach. If they share an experience, it's one of shame. In Spain, however, those same elites continue to bask in the glow—and continue to enjoy the spoils—of victory. And they wouldn't think twice to use force in order to preserve their privileges." Ironically, if the gap between Spain and Europe has been closing, Sirera said, it's less due to changes in Spain than to changes in Europe. "Spain's interpretative framework, which has long separated us from Western European democracies, is now bringing us closer to the new consensus emerging in the EU as it is adapting to meet the needs of the anti-Communist countries in the East—which includes the need to whitewash the fascist past of countries such as Croatia or the Ukraine."

Pablo Sánchez León, the historian, believes that the most widespread legacy of Francoism in Spain today is a phenomenon that he dubs a "double moral standard": the tendency "to present yourself publicly as the embodiment of standard democratic values while maintaining and reproducing in private, hidden from public scrutiny, a whole set of interests that flatly contradict those values." This double moral standard, he adds, is by no means limited to the political Right. "The phenomenon has less to do with ideology per se than with the tendency to undervalue collective political action, to passively accept authority and established norms at all levels." Another important factor is the tendency to "promote individual or group interests through informal channels and networks of friendship and social and relational capital"—in short, the form of nepotism that's known in Spain as *enchufismo* (literally, being plugged in). Sociologically, these holdovers from Francoism are not particular to Spain, Sánchez León points out. "The phenomenon of the double moral standard is common to all regimes that deprive their citizens of political freedoms and freedom of opinion. It thrives in the absence of any education in the values and practices of democratic citizenship." With the emergence of Vox, these subtle forms of sociological Francoism have coincided with more explicit forms of ideological Francoism, Sánchez León said. But, he added, "we shouldn't forget that sociological Francoism affects all political cultures, not just those on the right. Spanish Communism, for example, has been deeply marked by it as well." Incidentally, this double moral standard "jibes very well with a Catholic culture that continues to be socially dominant in a world that's already been modernized. Ironically, the political culture of Communism that emerges in the years of the dictatorship reproduces many of the practices of the Catholic Church, albeit at the level of a political sect, that is, to a less extensive degree and within a space that is more formally political."

For Sánchez León, few institutional spaces in Spain are more deeply marked by this double moral standard than the public university system. "This is because, institutionally, Spanish public universities, and publicly funded research, are not pluralist. They lack any kind of 'civil society.'" Instead, he said, they constitute "a territory dominated by state functionaries who spend their time divvying up among themselves public resources—resources that, moreover, have an exceptionally high return in the informal economy that makes up sociological Francoism." University faculty embody the Francoist double standard almost to perfection: "On the one hand, they claim to promote the public good through a commitment to academic quality, scholarly rigor, and scientific development. On the other, they undermine these values in their daily institutional lives, which are marked by influence trafficking, negative selection, and corruption." As a result, Sánchez León said, the university in Spain has become a factory of social inequality, "where a privileged minority has tenure, high salaries, and all the decision-making power, while a majority of faculty and researchers without power works for insufficient pay on temporary contracts."

FURTHER READING

On the long-lasting impact of Francoism on Spain's universities, see Claret Miranda (2006). For more on sociological Francoism, see Esteban, Etura, and Tomasoni (2019). A classic text that considers key aspects of Spain's recent history from a left-wing geopolitical perspective is Garcés (2012).

3

Ignacio Echevarría

"Two Centuries' Worth of Endemic Backwardness"

For a certain part of the Spanish Left, the Civil War has become a default explanation for almost every aspect of the political present, Ignacio Echevarría argued in November 2019 in a provocative essay about Alejandro Amenábar's film *Mientras dure la guerra* (*While at War*), which is set during the first weeks of the conflict. The Left's inability to let go of this paradigm, Echevarría pointed out, seriously distorts its view of Spain's many social and political challenges. Worse, it skews and debilitates the Left's tactics. To simply dismiss the Far-Right party Vox as a specter from the Francoist past, for example, is a dangerous mistake, he wrote. While it's true that many of Spain's problems, including Vox, have historical roots, most go back much further than the Francoist period. Other phenomena that progressives like to brand as Francoist, on the other hand, are in fact "of a radically new nature."

Echevarría, who was born in Barcelona in 1960, has long been one of Spain's most prominent literary critics. He wrote for *El País*, the country's newspaper of record, from

1989 until 2004, when he resigned after a conflict over a negative review of a novel published by the newspaper's own media conglomerate. As a freelance editor, Echevarría has been responsible, among other things, for the posthumously published work of his close friend Roberto Bolaño, the Chilean novelist. He also co-directs the cultural section of the online magazine *CTXT: Revista contexto*. I interviewed him in early 2020.

———————

You argue that a section of the Spanish Left is wrong to reduce the Spanish Right to its "Francoist pedigree." In reality, you say, Spain's right-wing parties are fully conversant with their European counterparts, whether they are neoliberal or neopopulist. I accept your point that not everything that looks Francoist is in fact a holdover from the dictatorship. But did you really mean to minimize the importance of what Vázquez Montalbán called sociological Francoism? Isn't the influence of Francoism still noticeable in a broad range of attitudes, patterns, reflexes, or views, not just among the Right but also among the Left?

Yes, of course it is. But how could it be otherwise? In Spain today there are at least two generations who came of age during Francoism. You can't expect power structures that were in place for forty years, along with the mentalities they excreted, to disappear without a trace, even if the dictatorship ended more than forty years ago. Francoism, moreover, was not an episodic phenomenon. It was the outcome of a long historical process, a drawn-out struggle among factions—in terms of class, culture, and national identity—whose tensions Francoism managed to repress but not to eliminate.

You're saying that what we call Francoism did not die in 1975, but also that much of it was born before 1936.

I sometimes get the impression that people assume too simple an opposition between the dictatorship and the Second Republic, as if we are talking about two separate historical eras. But the truth is that the Second Republic was exceptional—and ephemeral—in the grand scheme of nineteenth- and twentieth-century Spanish history, at least until the Transition. Jumping over those five Republican years—or, rather, crushing them—Francoism linked up with a long history of coup-happy military officers, *pronunciamientos*, civil warfare (the Carlist wars), autarky, absolutism, repression, injustices, and inequalities, all sustained by a plutocracy and a clergy that were as anachronistic as they were ruthless. What I am wondering is how much of what people take to be a legacy or residue of Francoism in that "broad range of attitudes, patterns, reflexes, or views" still present in Spanish society today—as you point out, among both the Right and the Left—isn't rather a legacy of two centuries' worth of endemic backwardness and paralysis, imbecility, submission, and violence. Anyone visiting the formidable exhibit of Goya's drawings at the Prado Museum comes out with a pretty good idea of the bedrock on which Francoism was built. The show gives enough evidence to suspect that the inheritance that the dictatorship bequeathed to us was not amassed after the Civil War but goes back as far as the War of Independence of 1808–13.

I see your point. But the fact that this backwardness and paralysis has lasted as long as it did has a historical explanation: the way the Spanish Transition was conducted. Consider the Spanish judiciary, which has been the subject of intense debate of late. Ignacio Sánchez Cuenca has called out the "formalism" of the courts, which consistently seem to privilege the letter over the spirit of the law, while Enric Juliana, quoting the Economist, *has denounced the "heavy-handed legalism" of the judiciary, for example in relation to Catalonia. Both point to a certain attitude among Spanish judges that diminishes their respect for fundamental rights, including the right to be elected as a parliamentary deputy. I'd say this attitude is a clear holdover from Francoism—and one that's perfectly explicable, given the strong continuity between Franco's judiciary and that of the democratic period.*

Of course. But, again, who'd be so naïve as to think that a legacy like that would cease to operate from one day to the next? At this point, moreover, we are no longer talking about a legacy but about DNA. In the best of cases, it'll take two more generations to get it out of our system. Don't forget that, in most of the world, including Europe, the culture of democracy is still a relatively young vegetation to sprout in our historical and cultural soil. With barely two centuries' worth of growth, its resilience is far from guaranteed, even in countries that have been luckier than the rest, such as England or France. Let alone countries with more anomalous histories, like Spain. In Spain, which had barely any Enlightenment to speak of, it took long for a bourgeoisie to emerge that was remotely comparable to those of the surrounding countries. And it was that bourgeoisie which introduced the liberal gene. Let's not forget, either, that Spanish democracy reaches maturity toward 2010, when the so-called "regime of 1978" begins to show its first visible cracks. But this is precisely when democracy is in global retreat and neoliberalism is launching a general assault on fundamental rights, which are crushed on multiple fronts, including the technological front. This happens everywhere in the world, even in those countries where democracy is most established.

The fact that neoliberalism meshes well with Francoism, or post-Francoism, is also clear from recent books by Antonio Maestre and Paul Preston. If anything defined the dictatorship in economic terms, they show, it was the urge to convert public goods into private capital, and to then mobilize that capital for political control. This leads me to another question about the sway over the media exerted by both the political and the corporate elites. As authors like Pascual Serrano have shown, the forty-some years of Spanish democracy have been heavily marked by a promiscuous ménage à trois among the political class, the media conglomerates, and the business and banking worlds. Is that promiscuity a holdover from Francoism, a creature of the development of Spanish democracy, or simply a feature of advanced capitalism?

Sorry to be repetitive, but I'll say it again: Francoism lasted forty years. In France, the Nazi occupation and the Vichy regime lasted only four. In Germany, national socialism ruled for barely twelve years. De Gaulle prudently glossed over the massive racket of collaboration with the Nazis. He also left untouched many of the privileges that were obtained or consolidated through that collaboration. The "German miracle" presided over by Audenauer was performed with the active participation of former Nazis in the country's economic and political structures.

Look, I don't mean to question the fact that Spain suffers from dysfunctions that are particular to this country. But I do think that what you call the promiscuous ménage à trois among the political class, the media conglomerates, and the business and banking worlds is, above all, a consequence of advanced capitalism. A form of capitalism that, in the case of Spain, could emerge from, and benefit by, the historical scourge that was the Franco dictatorship. But that doesn't make Spain an exception. Just look at Italy and Berlusconi.

Let's look ahead for a bit. The Transition of 1978 embodied—and was made possible thanks to—a specific attitude toward the past (the Second Republic, the Civil War, and Francoism), or rather a specific relationship between the newly democratic present and that past. Spain still faces major challenges, in economic, judicial, political, and territorial terms. Do you think that solving those challenges demands that the relationship between present and past be redefined? In other words, does Spain need a second Transition, or is the constant focus on the past a distraction?

Well, I wouldn't go as far as calling it a distraction. Still, as I suggested in my piece about Amenábar's film, I think that the struggle for the recovery of historical memory can, in some cases, come to operate as a kind of placebo for progressive politics. As I said earlier, two generations of Spaniards alive today came of age during Francoism. This goes a long way toward explaining certain recalcitrant attitudes, among other phenomena. But at least two generations were born after Franco's death. They grew up in a democracy.

To be honest, I don't think that our culture—Spanish culture and contemporary culture generally—pays all that much attention to the past, unless it's in an opportunistic or doctrinaire way. I don't mean to trivialize the drama and suffering caused by the scars that our Transition left, but I don't think those scars are a burden of any kind for the whole of Spanish society. At most, they affect a dwindling minority of the population.

You ask about redefining the present's relationship to the past. But who the hell has any type of relationship with the past at all? Do you really think the twenty-four-year-olds who can't tell you for sure who Franco was have such a relationship? Do you really think we can speak of any relationship to the past in the case of the young people who call for Catalan independence and who, conveniently indoctrinated, believe that the Civil War was fought between Spaniards and Catalans? Then there's another point. How do you begin to define a relationship to the past? From what perspective? Do the ghosts from the past stirred by Basque and Catalan nationalists include the flagrant collaboration with the Franco regime by their own economic elites?

As I wrote in my essay, I often get the impression that the Civil War operates as a kind of mythical correlate of Spanish political phraseology. It's a correlate that projects current conflicts and tensions onto the past, distorting them in the process. The Spanish Civil War was a class war—we shouldn't forget that for not even a minute. It was a class war much before being a conflict between "the two Spains," between the Republic and the monarchy, between Madrid and the periphery, or between Enlightenment and reaction. So, if we want to talk about the present's relationship with the Francoist past, or with the origins of the Civil War and the Second Republic, we first need to update the terms we use to describe all of that. The Spanish elites are capitalist much before they are Francoist. And, as I've said, hiding their true identity by reducing them to the mythological terms of the Civil War only benefits them.

Don't get me wrong. I have no problem with exhuming Franco from the Valley of the Fallen. What I do have a problem with is progressive politicians who capitalize on those symbolic gestures without even beginning to confront other, much more urgent questions. After all, whom does politics serve? For whom is it practiced? If you'd interview a random group of people on the street, how many Spaniards under forty-five could tell you what in the hell the Valley of the Fallen even is? Instead of discussing all the corny plans to turn that place into something different, why don't we invest in educational policies that will help students learn how and for what purpose it was built in the first place? I mean, what's next? Turning the Palace of El Escorial into a shopping mall to erase the sinister trace of King Philip II from Spanish history?

The tendency you signal is not limited to the Left. The Right, too, loves to dip into the past to explain the present. The current government, they say, has been installed through a "coup" from the "Popular Front"; they also like to credit Franco with Spain's economic "miracle" or even with the arrival of democracy after his death. This brings me to my final question: do you think this broad tendency to read the present in terms of historical continuities—positive for the Right, negative for the Left—is itself a Francoist legacy? Franco, after all, identified himself fully with the nation and its collective,

God-given destiny. And he was also fond of invoking an unchange-
able national character as a justification for his rule.

No, I don't think that's a Francoist legacy. Reading the literature from the turn of the century is enough to undermine that hypothesis, or at least to nuance it. The idea of
the "two Spains" clearly precedes Francoism, for example.
Moreover, the Transition—however failed you may think it
was—sought to leave behind precisely that explanatory paradigm, although it's true that it did not bother to dismantle its
underlying mechanisms. So no, I don't think that hypothesis is sound. The most specific legacy of Francoism, in my
opinion, lies in the way it managed to appropriate the entire
battery of national symbols: flag, anthem, folklore, religion,
cuisine, landscapes, monuments, even the Spanish language.
Francoism took this array of symbols and associated it, irrepa-
rably, with its nationalist ideology. By doing this, it made any
other form of identification with these symbols impossible.

The harm this operation did is impossible to gauge. If
you travel through France or England, you constantly see
national flags hanging from pubs or souvenir shops. In Spain,
if you spot a Spanish flag on any building that's not a city
hall, the first thing you think is that you are dealing with
a *facha*, a fascist. Thanks to Francoism, at least two generations of Spaniards were thoroughly "vaccinated" against
Spain. They did not want anything to do with it. This is
clear in the Generation of 1950, the so-called children of the
war. It wasn't that Spain didn't "sting" them, as Unamuno
famously said it stung him. They simply couldn't care less.

What Francoism did was to very seriously undermine
Spain's cohesion as a nation, a cohesion that was already

fragile and problematic to begin with. In practice, Francoism monopolized Spanish nationalist sentiment. This is one
of the main reasons why so many people overestimate the
extent to which Francoism is still alive and well. There is
a knee-jerk reaction that compels people to assume that a
citizen who lives in Ávila, Cáceres, or Murcia who hangs
a Spanish flag off his balcony as a response to the Catalan
demand for self-determination is a Francoist, when in fact
he may well consider himself a lifelong democrat—and,
yes, a patriot, too.

4

Guillem Martínez

"Spanish History Is Full of Bad Jokes"

The sharpest chronicler of Spanish politics grew up in Cerdanyola del Vallès, an industrial suburb of Barcelona, although he doesn't consider himself Catalan or, for that matter, Spanish. Born in 1965, Guillem Martínez has been part of the country's media landscape for many years. After several decades at *El País*, he now writes mostly for the online magazine *CTXT: Revista Contexto*, where his beat is Spanish and Catalan parliamentary politics. His three most powerful weapons as a journalist are his erudition (he has a degree in literary studies); his playful, idiosyncratic style; and his skepticism. This toolkit has allowed him to hold his own through political hurricanes like the Catalan crisis of 2017, which he covered on an almost daily basis, ruthlessly exposing the hypocrisy, incompetence, and opportunism on all sides. Among other books, Martínez is the editor of *CT, o, La cultura de la Transición* (2012), a groundbreaking volume that, in the wake of the 15M movement, critically outlined the limits of what could be said—or thought—in the first thirty-five years of post-Franco democracy. It was the first comprehensive cultural critique of the Regime of 1978. I spoke with Martínez in January 2020.

———————

Somewhere in the 1980s, Vázquez Montalbán popularized the concept of "sociological Francoism." What does that term mean to you?

If I remember correctly, Vázquez Montalbán lifted the phrase from a sociological study that was conducted or coordinated around the time Franco died by Isidre Molas, one of the founders of the Catalan branch of the Socialist Party. That study left a deep impression on the Spanish Left. Using surveys, it made clear that *el desarrollismo*, the rapid economic development promoted by the regime in the 1950s and '60s, had molded everyone and their mother. It also made clear that a sizeable part of Spanish society was in favor of order— something that is always imposed vertically—and therefore against risky adventures involving things like democracy, justice, or a redistribution of wealth. The only adventures they felt okay about, in other words, were those that are the staple of any nineteenth-century novel, the genre that gave a voice to the middle class: succeeding in life, overcoming difficulties, marriage, kids, and an escape to some faraway island.

What was shocking about the study, in other words, was that it proved that Francoism was sociologically real.

Yes; it proved that around the time when what we now call the Regime of 1978 was founded Francoism *existed*. And, I would add, that it existed in two different ways. On the one hand, it clearly existed formally: as manifested in the state and everything it stood for; in El Movimiento, Franco's party, which was much more than that and which consisted of several thousand individuals with a license to bear arms (and who did not get fully involved, as many had feared); and in the army, which, incidentally, got to write its very own set of articles for the 1978 Constitution without any interference from the politicians.

Speaking of the constitution, another conspicuously Francoist element in that document is its Preamble. It's not only quite sophisticated but also makes clear that some elements were simply not subject to negotiation between the regime and the democratic opposition. Let's not forget that the person who appears in that Preamble is the King—that is, the successor appointed by Franco himself. And he does so as the one who *grants* the Constitution to the citizenry. The Spanish Preamble is radically different from the one that precedes, for example, the Constitution of West Germany. The German Preamble speaks about, and reflects on, the fascist past of the German state, condemning that past and atoning for it, while positing democracy and the welfare state as the opposites of fascism. Tellingly, nothing like this happens in the Spanish text.

You were saying that the state, the Movimiento, and the Army are the first form in which Francoism existed in the late 1970s. What was the second?

The second is the informal or sociological Francoism that Vázquez Montalbán referred to. This kind of Francoism

[74]

came factory-installed, so to speak, in everyone who was
born in Spain between 1939 and some indeterminate point of
the democratic period. It's important, I think, to clearly dis-
tinguish between the formal and informal forms of Francoism. Both are born from violence, which means that both
are tainted. But they are different from each other, and
only one of them has a human face. To make things worse,
both are difficult to spot or even to define today. Because
both are, by now, mediated by the democratic culture that
evolved after Franco's death.

But do both continue to exert influence in Spain today?

This is the thing: I would say that, by now, this democratic
culture as it evolved after Franco's death is a more powerful force than Francoism in any of its forms.

What do you mean?

What I mean is that the pathology of Francoism in Spain
today—whether in a political sense or, on the opposite end,
a sociological sense—is determined *by the extent to which
Spanish culture assumes Francoism as part of normality*. Another
way to put this is to say that the pathology of Spain's democratic culture is its inability to think of itself as problematic in any way: its inability to explain its own problematic features and to acknowledge them as such. Features
that include its Francoism, its nationalism, or its vertical-
ity. What I am saying is that, looking at Spain's democratic culture today, that democratic culture itself is more of
a shaping force—and therefore more of a problem—than

Francoism. Which, I'm afraid, is actually worse than if it were the other way around.

But isn't Vox a Francoist party?

Yes, it is, and there are others. But here's the rub: Vox and these other parties define themselves as *democratic* and even, if you will, as anti-authoritarian. In other words, they take full advantage of Spain's democratic culture, which grants them the tremendous service of not having to vindicate the past. In any other democracy, the way Vox defines itself would be simply ridiculous. But not in the democratic culture that was forged in Spain in the 1970s and '80s.

Let's go back to Vázquez Montalbán's franquismo sociológico. Doesn't that informal manifestation of Francoism still shape attitudes, practices, or structures of power in Spain today?

In light of what I just explained, the answer would be: No, it does not. It's worse than that. The attitudes, practices, or power structures that shape Spain today are those that Spanish democracy adopted as *democratic* attitudes, practices, and power structures. Among all those, some precious Francoist gems survive, of course; but they are no longer exactly Francoist. By now, they are gems of Spanish democracy. That is to say, they have become part of the body of Spanish democracy.

There's something grotesque or tragic in the way you put that.

It's a bad joke, that's what it is. But Spanish history is full of bad jokes, so one more doesn't matter. What explains this one? It's not just the fact that Franco's dictatorship was fascist, or even that is was the only dictatorship from the 1930s that wasn't defeated and brought to justice but rather, thanks to the Cold War, normalized and accepted by the so-called Free World. No, what explains this bad joke, I would say, is an intimate political fact.

Intimate?

For those who have not experienced fascism first-hand, it's important to point out what makes it unique. Fascism doesn't just live in the state, or in the street, in stadiums, schools, factories, or on the radio, in the newspapers, and on television. Fascism also lives in your house. It moves in with you. Which explains Spain today.

How?

I'll try to explain it with a counterfactual. If the bad guys had come out winning in World War II, the history that we would have seen unfold in Europe in technicolor is the history that in fact unfolded in Spain, albeit in gritty black-and-white. Think Philip K. Dick's *The Man in the High Castle*, but worse. Hitler would have died in 1975. After his death, there'd have been a democratic transition, although it would have been limited in scope, not just by the presence of the recently disbanded NSDAP but also by the very souls of the politicians and voters, normalized as they would have been in decades of abnormality. A new European culture would have been created, liberated from its past, which would have been condemned sincerely—well, okay, more or less sincerely. Because the condemnation would not have fully invalidated that past; it would also have acknowledged certain positive achievements that everyone would agree on.

Like what?

I don't know, something like "Hitler was who he was, but he did create Europe's middle class." At the same time, people would refer to the fact that, while Nazism had been violent, there'd been a parallel and comparable violence emanating from the Jewish and Roma peoples, the Communists, the Social Democrats, and the liberals. Okay, now fast-forward forty-five years. By 2020 or so, we'd see Europe's first coalition government being formed. It's moderately social-democratic. It dares to discuss the past with a bit more intensity—but stays far from, say, anything resembling the Nuremberg trials. And it has one Jewish minister in the cabinet. The mass graves with bodies or ashes from the Nazi camps are not exhumed until the mid-twenty-first century. Why does it take so long? Not because of any lingering Nazism, of course not! No, the new democratic culture simply makes the choice not to poke around in the past.

There's your plotline. The story sounds absurd, doesn't it? Well, let me tell you, it's not quite as absurd if you live it every day, as we've had to in Spain.

You argue that key elements of Francoism have by now been fully assimilated into Spain's body politic, almost like shrapnel enveloped in scar tissue, or maybe rather like genetic flaws. But what exactly are those genetic flaws? How do they manifest in, say, the media or in political life?

I'd say they manifest in four ways: as an idea of nationalism, an idea of the state, an idea of centrality, and an idea of the common good.

Let's start with the first one, a notion of nationalism.

What I am referring to is the normalization—that is, the absorption into common sense—of a "natural" idea of Spain. One that posits Spain as a millenarian nation, going back even to pre-Roman times. This leads to a second normalization, also absorbed into common sense: the notion of Spain as a Catholic nation, albeit in implicit rather than explicit terms. This nationalism hails from the late nineteenth century: it doesn't go back further than Menéndez Pelayo, the reactionary founder of Spanish philology. The continued presence of this type of nationalism also illustrates one of the main achievements of Francoism. It managed to freeze-frame an idea of Spain that, in turn, was freeze-framed right after the failure of First Republic, in 1874—after the first democratic revolution in 1868—and the Restoration. All that freeze-framing explains why things sometimes get so cold down here, despite the sun.

How does this nationalism relate to your second element, an idea of the state?

In Spain, people generally don't make a distinction between the government and the state. For the Right, in particular, they are almost always one and the same thing. In Spain, moreover, the government and the state enjoy a surprising level of authority and prestige. This brings us to the third element: centrality.

Do you mean centralism, as opposed to federalism?

Not quite. What I am referring to is a double idea. First, the notion that politics is like the story of Goldilocks and the three bears: the idea that, in politics, there is a middle point, *un justo medio*, where things are just right, a very eighteenth-century concept. And second, that it is the government, especially a right-wing government, that represents that middle point, like a Napoleonic source of calibration or an atomic clock that broadcasts the exact time over short-wave radio.

Where does this notion come from?

I actually think it's is a fossil of Francoism. Which gives an indication of the fact that it's at bottom apolitical. It represents the aspiration not to get mixed up in politics.

I know what you mean. The old no te signifiques, *don't call attention to yourself, stay out of trouble, which often becomes citizens' modus operandi during a dictatorship. Mind your own business and you'll be fine; but if the regime is after you, you must have done something to provoke it.*

In the Francoist period, politics itself ended up stigmatized. So much so, let's not forget, that politics as we know it was in fact exterminated.

But are you saying that this demonization of politics in the name of common sense still survives in Spain today?

Yes, it does. Not only has it survived; it is assumed to be the common-sense position in both political life and in the media. The common-sense position serves to signal what's the correct way of thinking and acting. In reality, of course, it's a sense that's much less "common" than it is nationalist, conservative, even statist.

Statist?

I mean that it is a position that appears to rise above party interests. What's perceived as "political," on the other hand, is dismissed as partisanship. Something that's clashing, disturbing, unseemly.

Talk about the last of your four elements, the common good.

The three preceding elements all point to a notion of the common good, as determined by the government/state, which is good by definition and therefore should be respected by all, including the press and the cultural sector. To be critical or to point to problems, by contrast, is seen, even to some extent today, as unseemly and disturbing. Something that's unwanted, not proper. In short, a form of radicalism.

Ignacio Echevarría wrote in the fall of 2019 that, despite what some on the Left may think, the vestiges of Francoism are not, by any means, a central problem for Spain today. Emilio Silva, on the other hand, points to a Francoism-that-refuses-to-go-away as a persistent cause of Spain's many problems, a millstone around the country's neck. Which is it?

In all modesty, I don't think Francoism as such is the problem. What's problematic is its normalization or, in any case, Spain's inability to see it. The problem, in other words, is that Spain's democratic culture has normalized Francoism to such an extent that it is incapable of perceiving it any longer. This is in part because it lacks the tools for doing so. What Spain's democratic culture has looked for from the beginning is cohesion. It does not want to problematize anything.

So I agree with Ignacio, who's a friend of mine. There are problems in Spain whose origins precede Francoism, although Francoism prolonged them, normalized them, or reworked them into a baroque remix. But as I said earlier, to me the central phenomenon to understand Spanish politics today is the way Spanish politics freeze-framed itself in the periods 1874 to 1931 and 1939 to 1975—that is to say, over the hundred years between 1874 and 1975, with the five years from 1931 to 1936 as a brief interlude. This freeze-framing is the key to understanding Spanish politics today and, I'm afraid, the country's politics of the future.

What happened in those hundred years?

Things that should have occurred were prevented from taking place. Opposite things happened instead. On top of that, we were showered with a bunch of myths that are still alive and well today. It's over these hundred years that Spain's originality within Europe really takes shape. Traumatically so, I should add, because the country had a solidly innovative agenda.

Have things improved since 1975?

Yes, but there have been other problems. If you look at the way we talk about Francoism, for example, you'll notice that we do so with the grammar of democracy, so to speak, not with the grammar of fascism.

What do you mean?

What I mean is that the heirs of Francoism—its direct heirs, those who proudly claim its legacy—do not *talk* like José Antonio Primo de Rivera, or even like Franco. They talk like any other politician or journalist would. This, to me, indicates that the real problem resides in our democratic culture.

Which is Emilio Silva's point.

Emilio is a good friend as well. I agree with him that there are state structures, specifically the judiciary, in which the myths of the Restoration and Francoism have been allowed to thrive unchallenged. Worse, there are judges who clearly believe that is their mission to defend those myths tooth and nail, law in hand. And they defend them through something called *constitucionalismo*.

What's that?

It's the defense, to the death, of the Constitution of 1978, but with an added interpretative element: the interpretation that allowed José María Aznar to incorporate the Far Right—the Francoist Right—*into* the Constitution. Going out on a limb, I'll see Emilio's bid and raise the stakes: what the Right calls "constitutionalism" in fact has nothing to do with the Constitution. It's a reactionary interpretation of it, linked, on the one hand, to corruption rackets between the corporate world and the state but also, on the other, with sustaining myths that go back to Francoism or the late-nineteenth-century conservatism of Menéndez Pelayo.

And this is, I suspect, where centralism comes in, understood as an opposition to anything that resembles federalism in the name of a sacralized notion of the Spanish nation.

Yes. And what's worrisome, deeply worrisome, is that King Felipe VI supported that interpretation of the constitution in the televised speech he gave two days after Catalonia's failed referendum for independence, on October 3, 2017. Of course, the King has always read the constitution that way, as did his father, Juan Carlos I. But at the moment he gave that speech, at the height of the Catalan crisis, this interpretation implied the use of violence against a broad sector of Catalan society—something that, fortunately, did not end up happening.

Can you explain how this phenomenon of constitucionalismo *connects with your pessimistic view of Spain's democratic culture?*

What it comes down to is that in a country like Spain, a country with a recent fascist past, *constitucionalismo* allows for the creation of a very curious type of Far Right. It's a Far Right that thinks of itself as democratic. It believes in voting, for example, and it believes a government should respect the Constitution. But it is a respect for the Constitution *as interpreted by the Right,* whose reading of it is so intense that it excludes any other, more social or progressive interpretation from the outset. Which is nothing short of dramatic.

And this brings us back to the central problem. In the face of *constitucionalismo*, Spain's democratic culture is weak, powerless, incapable of defending itself. All it can do is stand by and watch. It accepts the Right's disturbing positions as normal and penalizes other points of view, dismissing and delegitimizing them as disturbing.

I understand your point that the problem is, by now, no longer any remnant from the Francoist past but the nature of Spanish democracy today. Still, even constitucionalismo *implies a particular relationship to the collective past. To what extent do you think that a conscious redefinition of that relationship to the past is an indispensable step for moving forward and addressing the country's problems?*

The past is always being redefined, as anyone who's been divorced will tell you. But when we talk about Spain's political past, it's clear that Spain's democratic governments over the past forty-some years have made ample use of a prerogative offered to them by Spain's political culture—that is, to impose, top-down, their view of society on that same society, in such a way that society perceives that view as the only authorized one.

In terms of the relationship to the past, or specifically to the civil war and the dictatorship, the successive governments headed by the Socialist Party have doubled down on the need to *overcome* the past. What they've offered in return to those who fought, and lost, against fascism is not justice but sentimentality. It's the recipe contained in Javier Cercas's novel *Soldiers of Salamis*. The governments of the PP, by contrast, have doubled down on the idea that "both sides committed excesses." For the Right, this is an incredibly productive notion because, first, it wipes the past clean and, second, it implies an unspoken coda: both sides committed excesses, *and therefore the best side won.*

The high point of the sentimentality offered by the PSOE was the 2007 Law of Historical Memory. Which, when you think of it, is the exact opposite of a Nuremberg trial. Rather than resolving the conflict from the past through justice, it simply drowns it in sentimentality, imposed once again in the top-down manner that's so ingrained in Spanish political culture.

How should the government, or the state, deal with the continued lack of consensus about the Civil War and Francoism? The measures of the last year or so, from Franco's exhumation to the question of what to do with the Valley of the Fallen or the proposal to include extolling Francoism into the criminal code, have all been controversial, even among the Left.

Personally, I do not think it's the government's job to teach history lessons. Spanish governments have been telling us how to understand our history for a hundred years. It's time they stopped doing that. When it comes to the past, the

parliament should adopt effective laws based on internation-
ally accepted notions of democracy and human rights—
laws that compensate for the absence in Spain of anything
resembling a Nuremberg trial. What should *not* be done is
to further sentimentalize things. We don't need to place
any more wreaths anywhere. Nor, even, is it necessary to
remove Francoist symbols from public spaces. Rather than
taking anything away, what we should do is add plaques
that explain that yes, fascism existed here, and that it was,
in fact, the only European form of fascism to win the war.

How about penalizing the extolment of Francoism?

I don't think it's a good idea to use the criminal code to limit
freedom of speech. What *is* necessary, on the other hand,
is to annul the political convictions issued by the Francoist
courts, much like Germany did in its day. This measure
would imply a de-authorization of Francoism. Francoism
would finally be expelled from democracy. Up until now,
Francoism survives in those death and prison sentences.
Those convictions are part of the legislative corpus of the
state today. As such, they express the idea that Francoism
was legitimate. They underscore the *continuity of the state*
from Francoism to our current democracy—a democracy
whose essence then becomes the very continuity of that state.

And that continuity is the problem: that which Emilio Silva describes
as the millstone around Spain's neck.

To rid ourselves of that millstone, the state must be *discontin-*
ued, to begin with in juridical terms. To be sure, this is less

dramatic of a task than it would have been in the 1970s. Still, something tells me that even the current coalition government will not go that far, despite what the PSOE may have promised during its election campaign. They may well revert to swapping out actual annulment with a new dose of sentimentality for the individuals who were sentenced. By which they'd avoid, once more, any real break with the Francoist state.

To have a sense of what that might look like, we need to look no further than Catalonia. In June 2017, the regional parliament passed a law that, it claimed, annulled the political convictions from the Francoist period, affecting some sixty-four thousand sentences issued between 1938 and 1978. But this was bogus: a parliament doesn't have the power to annul judicial sentences. Can you imagine? No corrupt politician would ever land in jail! No, what a parliament *can* do, as it did in Germany, is to pass a law that obliges the courts to annul a sentence if and when the person convicted, or their heirs, requests such an annulment. But this was not what happened in Catalonia. Instead, the regional government performed a kind of magic trick. Those convicted simply received a diploma from the government, with a Catalan flag and an official seal, that stated that their conviction had been annulled, which was false. Voilà, problem solved.

Personally, I don't think the current central government is going to do much better. They won't have the guts to actually annul any conviction, either. The last mass annulment in Spanish juridical history in occurred in September 1939, when Franco voided the thousands of divorces that occurred after the Second Republic legalized divorce for the first time in modern Spanish history. And there's another part to this.

By offering sentimentality instead of annulment when it comes to the political convictions of the Francoist years, the government would reduce the issue to a culture war, a field in which the Right always holds the home advantage.

To complicate things further, the whole issue of annulment is not limited to moral reparation. There's an important material aspect to the question as well.

Yes, that's right. We should not forget that fascism sought not just to eliminate its political rivals, but to profit from that elimination. In Spain, the benefit often consisted in the house or the land of the person executed. This, too, is why any measure or policy that replaces annulment and reparation with sentimentality would be a swindle. It'd fit Spain's democratic culture to a tee.

5

The Judiciary

"The harsh reality of history": that's how Spain's Constitutional Court referred to Franco's victory in the Spanish Civil War. The judges invoked the phrase in 1982 to justify a decision denying Juan Bautista Santaella his right to the benefits deriving from his military service. Santaella had voluntarily enlisted with the Republican army in September 1936, two months after the failed military coup of Franco and his fellow officers had unleashed a civil war. He'd been promoted to corporal by December and to sergeant by the following summer. In February 1939, as the Republic's defenses were crumbling, he'd crossed the French border along with thousands of fellow soldiers and found himself interned in a French concentration camp.

Forty years later, in August 1979, he filed a request with the Ministry of Defense to be reinstated as a member of the Armed Forces with all the attending benefits—benefits denied to him by the Francoist legislation, for which active defense of the Republic against the 1936 coup was defined as an act of treason. The request, which was initially denied, confronted the Constitutional Court with a complicated question: to what extent did Francoist jurisprudence continue to trump Republican legality, even after Franco's death and the adoption of the Constitution in 1978?

In a landmark decision, the Court confirmed the primacy of Francoism over the Republic, even under Spain's new democratic Constitution. After all, the verdict argued, the decrees to which Santaella was appealing "were never in force in the territory dominated by those who had risen up in arms against the Republican institutions, whose legitimacy they denied." "This," the Court concluded, deploying the phrase I quoted above, "is the harsh reality of history": clearly, Franco's victory established a new "legal regime" (*ordenamiento jurídico*), establishing a comprehensive break with the preceding legality. What the Court's verdict also underscored, however, is that if the Franco regime established such a break with the legality preceding it, the transition to democracy following Franco's death clearly did not (Boletín Oficial del Estado 1982; Aragoneses 2017; Baylos Grau 2008).

Thirty years later, the Spanish judiciary had another important opportunity to reconsider its position. In February 2012, the Supreme Court issued a verdict in the case brought against Judge Baltasar Garzón. Garzón achieved world fame in the late 1990s as a champion of universal jurisdiction, prosecuting former military leaders and heads of state responsible for state violence and the systematic violation of human rights in the Southern Cone, among other places. Ten years later, in October 2008, Garzón finally turned that bold human-rights lens inward toward his own country. In his role as investigative magistrate at Spain's national Criminal Court (Audiencia Nacional), he initiated an investigation of presumed crimes against humanity—including tens of thousands of cases of forced disappearance—committed by the rebel forces and their supporters following the 1936 coup against the Second Republic. A month later, once Garzón had formally established that the thirty-five military and political leaders mentioned by name in his initial indictment were deceased, the judge took a step back and delegated the further pursuit of the cases of forced disappearance to regional courts.

Although Garzón had only pursued the case for a month, his unprecedented approach had attracted worldwide media attention and stirred up a major controversy in the legal world and beyond. It wasn't long before three Spanish Far-Right organizations charged him with "perversion of justice" (*prevaricación*), claiming he had knowingly pursued a case that ignored established law, specifically the general amnesty of 1977. What made the indictment possible in the first place was a curious figure in the Spanish legal system, the so-called *acusación popular*, which allows any party to bring charges even if it is not directly affected by the presumed criminal activity. As it turned out, the three accusing parties found a willing ear, and even a helping hand, in the Spanish judiciary, which seemed to welcome the opportunity to rid itself of one of its most visible members. And given the fact that Garzón was a judge himself, his case was tried before the Supreme Court.

Once more, one of the country's highest judicial powers faced an existential question: did the country's obligations established by international law—for which crimes against humanity don't prescribe and are not subject to

amnesty—outweigh its adherence, first, to Francoist jurisprudence and, second, to the Amnesty Law? Once again,
the court confirmed continuity. Although the verdict finally cleared Garzón of the charge of perversion of justice,
the seven magistrates who signed the opinion left no doubt
as to the larger existential question. On the one hand, the
Court affirmed that the citizens who had brought the case
to Garzón had a right to truth: they were entitled to find
out what happened to their missing family members. On
the other, though, the Court argued that the criminal justice system was not the proper channel to satisfy that right.
They wielded four reasons for this position: the time that
had passed since the alleged crimes; the fact that the perpetrators were dead; the fact that no law can be applied ret-
roactively; and the nature of the Spanish transition. "The
method of judicial investigation," the judges wrote, "is not
that of the historian. . . . [W]hile the differences between
memory and history are self-evident, so, too, are those that
exist between history and the results of a judicial investigation undertaken with a different goal than that pursued
by the historian" (Tribunal Supremo 2012, 10).

It's hard to exaggerate the consequences of this Supreme
Court verdict. For one, it effectively closed off the entire
Spanish legal system to any further demands from Franco's
victims. Second, its invocation of the general amnesty to do
so was highly suspect, critics have argued. For even if a crime
may be subject to amnesty, it can only be marked as such
after it is properly investigated. As Rafael Escudero has written, the court "rejected the international legal doctrine that
establishes a duty to investigate the fate of the disappeared,
even if it is not possible to punish those who are guilty

because of amnesty or prescription. Under international law, the judiciary has the obligation to satisfy the right to truth that belongs to victims of alleged or established human rights violations" (2014, 124–25). Others have pointed out that the verdict betrays its ideological bias through its use of suspect terms to describe Spanish history, including the phrase *los dos bandos* (the two sides) to describe the Civil War (Jiménez Villarejo and Doñate Martín 2012, chapter 8).

"Garzón was punished," the journalist Ignacio Escolar said, "for not obeying a prohibition": "There is an unwritten pact among the big powers [of the state] that Francoism is a secret garden you cannot enter. . . . And anyone who breaks that taboo must be punished" (Bosch and Escolar 2018, chapter 6). Meanwhile, with all Spanish avenues to legal justice blocked, one group of victims resorted to an Argentine court to seek justice. Ironically, they successfully appealed to the same principle of universal jurisdiction that Garzón had invoked in his groundbreaking prosecution of heads of state in the 1990s. The story of the so-called *querella Argentina* is told in the award-winning documentary *El silencio de otros* (Carracedo and Bahar, dirs., 2018; *The Silence of Others* [2019]).

The Supreme Court's 2012 decision in the Garzón case also helped bring home the weaknesses and lacunae of the Law of Historical Memory that had been adopted in the intervening years. Officially titled the "Law that recognizes and broadens the rights and takes measures in support of those who suffered persecution or violence during the Civil War and the dictatorship," the law, as we saw earlier, established modest monetary reparations for victims of Francoist repression and their family members; promised state help in the exhumation of mass graves; prohibited the presence of Francoist symbols in public spaces (plaques, street names statues, etc.); proscribed any political use of the Valley of the Fallen (the massive monument where Franco was buried); granted Spanish citizenship to former members of the International Brigades and to children and grandchildren of Spanish Republican exiles; and turned the Spanish Civil War Archive in Salamanca into a Center of Historical Memory.

Juridically more important, however, was the fact that the new law stopped short of annulling Francoist jurisprudence. To be sure, the law declared "illegitimate" and "radically unjust" "the courts, juries, and whatever other penal or administrative organs that, during the Civil War, were established to impose, for political or ideological reasons or reasons of religious faith, sentences or sanctions of a personal character," explicitly including the verdicts issued by the regime's most central political courts: the Court to Repress Freemasonry and Communism, the Court of Public Order, and the Courts for Political Responsibilities and War Councils. The memory law applied the same notion of illegitimacy to any convictions resulting from individuals' support for the Republic or their struggle for the return of democracy to Spain. But despite all this, it did not systematically annul any verdict—a measure that the United Nations has urged Spain to adopt. Instead, the law merely recognized the right for individuals to seek a declaration repairing their honor (Boletín Oficial del Estado 2007). The United Nations has been pressing the Spanish state for several years to comply with the International Covenant on Civil and Political Rights, which the country ratified more than forty years ago. In 2015, the UN Human Rights committee stated that the amnesty law should be annulled because it "hinders the investigation of past human rights violations, particularly crimes of torture, enforced disappearance and summary execution" (United Nations Human Rights Committee 2015, 6–7; Faber 2018, 86–87) As we saw earlier, the new Law of Democratic Memory that Spain's progressive coalition government proposed in September 2020 does not contemplate annulling the amnesty law.

In the more than four decades since the adoption of the 1978 Constitution, the lack of a clean break with Francoist legality has led to a long list of other controversial court decisions. In large part thanks to the memory movement, however, Spanish public opinion has been increasingly less tolerant of them, as some recent cases show.

In May 2019, María del Rosario Campesino Temprano, a judge of the Provincial Court of Madrid, slapped Teresa Rodríguez with a €5,000 fine for libel. According to the judge, Rodríguez, who at the time was a deputy for Podemos in the regional parliament of Andalusia, had "harmed the right to honor" of José Utrera Molina, who had served as minister in one of Franco's last cabinets (Rocha 2019), and who had died in April 2017. What had happened? In March 2018, Rodríguez had posted a tweet that said, "Forty-four years ago today, Salvador Puig Antich was executed by *garrote vil*. Among those responsible for his assassination [were Manuel] Fraga, who founded the PP, and Utrera Molina, [who] was buried last year to the tune of Cara al Sol, sung by members of the same party. They keep going, but so do we." Accompanying the tweet was a four-minute segment of the film

Salvador (Puig Antich) (Burns, dir., 2006) that re-enacted the
scene from March 1974 in which the then twenty-five-year-
old Catalan anarchist was executed shortly after receiving
a death sentence. Rodríguez's tweet also referenced the funeral of Utrera Molina, which had taken place in April 2017
in the presence of Alberto Ruiz-Gallardón of the Partido
Popular, former minister of Justice and mayor of Madrid,
who, as it happened, was also Utrera Molina's son-in-law.
At the funeral, a group of men sang the Falangist hymn
"Cara al sol" (LaSexta 2017).

It was the Utrera Molina family who, a year later,
brought the charge of libel against Rodríguez (Riveiro and
Escribano 2018). The judge ruled in their favor, arguing
that to call Utrera Molina "responsible" for the "assassination" of Puig Antich was an "offense" to the deceased and
therefore manifested a lack of "respect for the pain of the
family caused by the loss of a loved one." The judge also
argued that Rodríguez had falsely characterized Puig Antich's death as an assassination. Puig Antich's 1974 death sentence, which the cabinet Utrera Molina was part of could
have commuted, "followed the legislation then in force,"
the judge wrote. If Utrera Molina held any responsibility,
it was merely "political" in nature (Bocanegra 2019). Critics
were quick to point out that the judge's verdict appeared to
justify what in effect had been the execution of a political
dissident by a dictatorial regime, making it appear as if Puig
Antich's trial had taken place under the rule of law (Bocanegra 2019). To make things worse, the legal scholar Joaquín
Urías pointed out, the judge's opinion privileged the family's right to honor over Teresa Rodríguez's constitutional
rights, in particular her right to freedom of speech (2019).

This wasn't the first time that reputational concerns were invoked to smother or censure public debate about the dictatorship and its legacies. In his book *Shoot the Messenger?* (2013), the historian Francisco Espinosa Maestre details thirteen cases in which Spanish courts prevented information about Francoist repression from becoming public. As Rafael Escudero, a professor of judicial philosophy, writes in his prologue to the book, the judges in question "have not hesitated to interpret [the] supposed 'right to honor' in a nearly categorical fashion, placing it above other fundamental rights such as freedom of expression and freedom of information" (2013, xviii). The irony is obvious: "It is indeed grotesque that people who represent and vindicate the honor of those who actively participated in the repression of a democratic regime like the Spanish Republic are now the first to turn to the Constitution and its fundamental rights—which were ignored during the Franco dictatorship—for their defense" (Escudero 2013, xvii–xviii).

Decisions like the one in the Rodríguez case, which will be appealed before the country's Supreme Court (Bocanegra 2020), hurt the legitimacy of the court system and feed the narrative that paints the Spanish state as fatally tainted by its Francoist origins (Faber 2020). "Can you imagine a judge condemning someone for calling a Nazi minister of government who signed death sentences an assassin?" Miguel Urbán Crespo, a member of the European Parliament for Podemos, tweeted. "In Germany this is impossible, but in Spain it is possible and today it happened once again. It's called impunity for Francoism" (2019). Urías, a former lawyer for the Constitutional Court and currently professor of constitutional law, tweeted that the decision was "unacceptable" (2019).

In light of cases like these, it is no surprise that the Spanish courts have an image problem. The population's faith in the judiciary is low. As mentioned earlier, in the spring of 2019 more than half of Spaniards responding to an EU poll expressed doubts about judicial independence in their country, placing Spain fourth lowest among all EU member states surveyed. To be sure, the judicial community is aware of the problem, and there have been strong voices from within calling for reform. In a scathing 2012 book, for example, two senior jurists, Carlos Jiménez Villarejo and Antonio Doñate Martín, critically inventoried the many ways the Spanish judiciary after 1978 has continued to be shaped by Francoism—what Josep Fontana, in the prologue, calls "the dark side of the real democracy in which we've lived since the Transition" (Fontana 2012).

Jiménez Villarejo is a former public prosecutor and Doñate Martín is a former judge and law professor. From their years of experience in the system, they note the persistent presence of "a Francoist ideological bias" that manifests in different ways and has lingered throughout the democratic period: "Francoism, including its authoritarian and anti-democratic foundations, is still with us" (2012, Epilogue). While some prominent members of the judiciary clearly hold Far-Right views, the systematic problems are of a more general nature. Spanish judges, they point out, for example, have not only tended to assume as given the legitimacy of the Franco regime and the illegitimacy of the Republican juridical order that preceded it, but they have also tended to associate democracy with "insecurity and disorder in all spheres of society" (2012, chapter 1). Yet the authors also highlight important signals of disagreements, sometimes expressed in dissenting judicial opinions. In 2006, for instance, when the Constitutional Court rejected out of hand a request from a woman to overturn the sentence of her father, who had been condemned by a Francoist court in 1942, one judge issued an opinion in which he stated that "In a just state . . . there is no room for sentences passed without a fair trial" (chapter 2).

In a more recent book that appeared soon after the escalation of the Catalan crisis, in which the judicial system played a central role, the journalist Ignacio Escolar and the judge Joaquim Bosch converse about some of the same problems, focusing on what they call "the judicialization of politics" and "the politicization of the judiciary." The reaction of the Spanish government, then headed by the conservative Partido Popular, to the massive civil-society protests in the wake of the Great Recession, they write, have initiated what can only be described as a regressive tendency that, among other things, has seriously eroded civil liberties such as freedom of expression (Bosch and Escolar 2018, Introduction).

They also call attention to other structural problems, including a lack of judicial independence that derives, first, from the fact that every new government gets to appoint a new attorney general (fiscal general del Estado) and, second, from the way judicial appointments and promotions are determined. These are controlled by a twenty-member central council, el Consejo General del Poder Judicial, whose members are appointed by Congress. This system was instituted in the 1980s, driven by the awareness of the need for a renewal of personnel in a still very Francoist judiciary. Yet in practice it has given Spain's largest political parties an undue influence over the court system and cleared the way for key appointments to become a matter of political horse-trading. Worse, judges have internalized the idea that, in order to have a successful career, it is less necessary to perform at the highest level than to win politicians' favor. "The general perception in the judiciary," Bosch recounts, "is that a judge may well be the best in his or her specialty, but that they will never be appointed to the Supreme Court if they do not achieve the support of one of the political parties. It's a very demoralizing feeling." Surveys show that 80 percent of Spanish judges believe that judicial appointments are not based on capacity or experience. Granting the legislative branch control over the judicial branch was a "patch instead of a real solution," Escolar concludes. And in recent years, the situation has only worsened (Bosch and Escolar 2018, chapter 2).

Bosch and Escolar also address the problematic status of the Audiencia Nacional, the central criminal court in Madrid that, as mentioned earlier, evolved directly from Franco's Court of Public Order (Tribunal de Orden Público), and whose remit includes large corruption cases, crimes against the monarchy, terrorism, financial crimes, drug trafficking, and international crimes. For Escolar, the Audiencia's main problem from a juridical point of view is that "it clashes with the spirit of a fundamental human right, namely the right to a natural judge." In fact, it's thanks to the presence of the Audiencia that the Spanish Constitution does not mention this right explicitly but rather speaks of a right to be tried by the "judge predetermined by the law" (chapter 2).

The twin problems signaled by Bosch and Escolar—the politicization of justice and the judicialization of politics—have

been on full display during the territorial crisis that sur-
rounded Catalonia's attempt in October 2017 to organize a
referendum for independence. The saga began in 2007 when
the Partido Popular took to the Constitutional Court to appeal Catalonia's new Statute of Autonomy, and ended, for
now, in the Supreme Court conviction of a group of Catalan
politicians and citizen activists for "sedition." Throughout,
commentators and legal scholars have questioned fundamental aspects of the process, including, once again, the role
of the Audiencia Nacional. It was a trumped-up charge of
"rebellion"—of which the accused were ultimately cleared—
that justified moving the trial to the Audiencia in Madrid
in the first place, instead of holding it in a Catalan court.
"Speaking off the record," Escolar reveals, "many jurists admit that the real reason [for the move to Madrid] was the
desire to avoid that the case be handled by a Catalan judge"
(chapter 5).

Finally, Bosch and Escolar criticize the Law of Historical
Memory from 2007 and the Supreme Court's interpretation
of that law, along with the general amnesty, to block any
judicial investigation of Francoist crimes. "The investigation opened by Baltasar Garzón sparked an intense internal debate in the judiciary," Bosch recalled, "even among
the progressive sectors, where . . . some of us thought that
investigating [the regime's] crimes should be possible." German and French courts, after all, tried Nazi war criminals
many years after the end of the Second World War. Moreover, "it was pertinent to wonder why [Spanish] judges
. . . could convict leaders of the Argentine dictatorship but
not those of the Spanish dictatorship." The juridical status
of the 1977 Amnesty Law, moreover, is less solid than the

Supreme Court made it seem, Bosch pointed out, given that it was approved by the Spanish parliament before the adoption of the Constitution. "The root of the problem," Bosch concludes, "is that all democrats should be able to unite in their rejection of Francoism. There should be a consensus to condemn the dictatorship unambiguously and to support granting reparations to its victims." The reason this hasn't happened in Spain is simple, he adds: "There is a very broad sector of Spanish society that would never define itself as antifascist. This would be unthinkable in Germany, Italy, France or the United States. We are the only country in Europe where one can declare oneself to be a democrat without also declaring oneself to be an antifascist" (chapter 6).

FURTHER READING

In addition to the highly readable critical analyses of Bosch and Escolar (2018) and Jiménez Villarejo and Doñate Martín (2012), both cited in this chapter, see Clavero (2019) for a critical account of the Spanish judiciary. For more on the role of the Spanish courts in relation to transitional justice, see Andrés Ibáñez (2015) and Martín Pallín and Escudero (2008). For a brief English-language overviews of Spain's political institutions in a comparative perspective, see Colomer (2020), Field (2020), and Garoupa and Magalhães (2020).

6

Sebastián Martín

"A Brake on Democratic Culture"

Sebastián Martín, who teaches legal history at the University of Sevilla, has written extensively on the history of Spanish legal thought and constitutionalism. Born in Sevilla in 1976, he is co-editor, with Rafael Escudero, of *Fraude o esperanza: 40 años de la Constitución* (Scam or hope: 40 years of the Constitution). I interviewed him in late 2019.

––––––––––

Although the transition to democracy allowed many people in power to stay put, the legalization of the opposition parties resulted in at least a partial renewal of personnel. This was not the case for the judiciary or the university, where fresh blood and ideas were much slower to enter.

That's right. In both there was an overwhelming sense of continuity. But this did not mean that by the time democracy arrived, the entire judiciary and university were

Francoist. In both, by then, there existed a small but consistent and relevant nucleus of democratic opposition. That said, it's true that the Francoist block that dominated both the universities and the courts, with all its propensities and bad habits, continued to be present and exercise an influence that in some ways is still noticeable today.

Can you say something more specific about the nature of the legacy of these blocks?

I can speak to two very specific legacies, the first one of which is present in the culture of the Spanish university, while the second one straddles the country's Schools of Law and judicial courts. The first has to do with the way our collective past has been instituted symbolically. The question here is not so much that, let's say, the high-school curriculum may grind to a halt at the coup of 1936 or, to the contrary, cover the twentieth century through the Transition while fully respecting the "equidistant" narrative instituted during the dictatorship, along the lines of "we all carried part of the blame." No, what I am talking about is the fact that the dominant public representations of our past— whether it's the period from the late nineteenth through the first third of the twentieth century, or projecting further back to the fifteenth century—are still those forged by the victors of the Civil War.

Where do you see the influence of these Francoist narratives?

They still shape both the frameworks adopted by academic historians and the public's perceptions of the past.

For example, it's still common to associate the Republican years with notions of chaos and violence, while the memory of the properly Republican project to modernize Spain, which was not quite leftist and not at all Communist, largely continues to be buried, as the exile writer Max Aub pointed out when he visited the country in the late 1960s. Buried, too, is the imperialist dimension of the Spanish war, which in most of the country's territory wasn't really a "civil" war at all, as Francisco Espinosa has repeatedly argued. In most of the country, the war was above all a kind of great massacre that served to found the new state, a massacre made up of war crimes and crimes against humanity. A third aspect that remains largely unknown are the close parallels between Francoism and other European forms of totalitarianism. People are still surprised to hear that Spain had concentrations camps and policies of extermination.

Francoism, in other words, was not an authoritarian, paternalist, Catholic system that went through a brief initial period of totalitarian contagion. Rather, it was a totalitarian dictatorship that saw itself forced to adapt to a democratic environment in order to survive. But that did not mean that it sacrificed its fundamental, antidemocratic tenets, which in fact informed its rule until the end. Regarding the preceding centuries, what's being buried is the fact that the Spanish monarchy was pluralist from its birth—a pluralism that's incompatible with the silly notion of Spain as "Europe's oldest nation." And then there's the criminal dimension of Spain's expansion into the Americas.

But haven't academic historians long disproved most of these myths?

Yes, of course, after forty years of democracy, there is plenty of powerful, well-researched historical scholarship that provides a counterweight to these narratives. And yet the Francoist legacy has persisted. To the detriment, I would add, of our democratic health. It would be desirable if the hegemony of those narratives could be displaced by more nuanced versions of our collective past, narratives that are not only more historically sound but also better fit to our constitutional democracy, and better fit to inspire our political decisions today. In that sense, the persistence of Francoist frameworks acts as a brake on the development of Spain's democratic culture.

You also spoke of a second legacy, which you said straddles law schools and the court system.

This legacy is almost more treacherous than the first, because it tries to pass itself off as something that fully adheres to our constitutional, democratic state. What I am referring to is a juridical culture that is dominant in our law schools and courts, which holds that a democracy should institute itself simply through the "rule of law," a phrase interpreted in the sense that the law reigns supreme. To be sure, this doctrine appears to be democratic and respectful of citizens' rights. Yet by glossing over any nuanced understanding of the social function of the law, or the actual content of the law, it's often used to dress up authoritarian or pre-constitutional responses from the courts to some of the most sensitive challenges we face. This juridical culture is a prime example of sociological Francoism.

Where did it originate?

Like many of the other manifestations of sociological Francoism, this one, too, is born long before the Civil War. It was quite present in the nineteenth-century liberal state and after the Restoration of 1874. Prominent intellectuals like José Ortega y Gasset and Fernando de los Ríos already complained about the way in which the dogma of "obeying the law" prompted authoritarian responses to the crisis of 1917. At that point, the dogma was invoked to justify the violent repression of labor unions and separatists, whose actions, such as a general strike, were labeled as "rebellion" rather than as a legitimate expression of disagreement with the existing order.

How did it change after Franco came to power?

The more strictly Francoist legacy in this interpretation of the notion of the *rule of law* lies in the fact that the Franco regime adopted precisely the same notion to legitimize itself toward the democratic West. By doing so, it nominally replaced the transcendental, scholastic, theological legitimacy that it had invoked in the wake of the 1936 coup and in the postwar years. But of course this move was little more than window dressing—the same kind of window dressing we still see today when the courts wield a pseudo-juridical argument based on this dogmatic interpretation of the rule of law, without taking into account, say, international human rights law or, for that matter, our own Spanish constitution. It's these same pseudo-juridical arguments that are wielded time and again in response to demands for judicial accountability regarding the crimes committed by the forces of order during the dictatorship, or even after Franco's death.

7

Ricardo Robledo

"Yes, We Are Still Different"

Ricardo Robledo, born near Salamanca in 1946, is a retired professor of economic history at the University of Salamanca and currently affiliated with the Pompeu Fabra University in Barcelona. He's worked extensively on agrarian history, including agrarian reform in the years of the Second Republic, and is the founder and editor of *Conversación sobre la historia*, a popular blog that features longform articles on historical topics of broad public interest. This interview is from late 2019.

———————

You studied at the Autonomous Universities of Madrid and Barcelona in the late 1960s. How was that?

The dominant atmosphere was less one of sociological Francoism than of sociological *anti*-Francoism. The Autonomous University of Barcelona was probably a special

case in this regard, given how it was created in 1968. I remember that, during the year 1968–69, in the Faculty of
Philosophy and Letters there was only one professor with
a Francoist air, Carlos Seco Serrano. Although he was eru-
dite and tolerant, he fueled a compact opposition and lasted
just one year. Speaking as a historian, those of us who went
through college in the early 1970s believed that any scholarship worth its salt was necessarily anti-Francoist. And we
did scholarship to bring about social change.

In that sense, did you experience the Transition as a disappointment?

Manuel Vázquez Montalbán said it well when, in an article
that came out in *La Calle* in May 1978, he wondered, with
a pun: "¿Contra Franco vivíamos mejor?" ["Were we better off when we lived against Franco?"; the pun reworks
the nostalgic phrase *Con Franco vivíamos mejor*, "We were
better off under Franco."] That article of his ended on a
prophetic note: "I sometimes have the impression that our
politicians, even the most honest among them, are saying
mass, in Latin, for a deaf-and-dumb congregation whose
members are slowly leaving the church." In other words,
even before the Transition was canonized, Vázquez Montalbán already put a finger on the skepticism that began to
dominate the general mood. The Transition, it seemed, was
little more than a pact among professionals that left the bulk
of the citizenry out of the loop.

*By then, the notion of disillusionment had been in the air for a while,
no? The film of that name,* El Desencanto, *by Jaime Chávarri,
is from 1976.*

Yes, that movie about the Panero family had followed on the euphoria of the preceding spring. There was a sense of longing for the feeling that comes with fighting for a set of clear objectives, despite the risks. Every spring has its moment of letdown.

As a member of that generation, how are you experiencing the new wave of critique of the Transition?

For those of us who are the survivors of that "sociological anti-Francoism," the disappointment can only be corrected through a Second Transition. History repeats itself, but not in the same way. Still, those of us who mobilized politically fifty years ago—at least, I'd say, those of us who did so in Catalonia—have a well-developed sensibility for detecting Francoist traces in a good part of today's political Right. These traces are more than the "whiff of mothballs" that Aitor Esteban of the Basque Nationalist Party mentioned in a recent newspaper piece. The gene has mutated, to be sure, moving toward the new forms of global, right-wing populism. But here in Spain its ideological anchor is still Francoist.

What would a Second Transition look like?

It's a two-sided coin. On the one side, the Second Republic functions as a moral reference point. This was completely absent in the Transition of 1978; if anything, in fact, at that point the Republic was a source of shame. On the other side, the road to the Second Transition will be less one of reform and more one of rupture, but only if Catalonia is taken into account. The reference point there will be the explicit rejection of Francoism.

Is Spain different, as Manuel Fraga, then a member of Franco's cabinet, famously said in the 1960s?

My short answer is yes. A significant section of conventional historiography has rejected this notion as a mere Francoist slogan. Spain, they said, is a normal country by now. José Álvarez Junco and Juan Pablo Fusi have made this point insistently. But they are wrong, at least with regard to the Transition as it's continuously invoked to attack the memory movement. The machinery of the Regime of 1978 is rusted and defective, and this is due to its original sin: the fact that the victors of the Civil War granted themselves amnesty. Franco established a radical break with the Republic. The Transition did nothing to change this. In terms of institutional memory, the Republican years were a black hole. The portrait gallery of government ministers ended in April 1931; the next portrait was a Francoist minister. As if the Republic hadn't existed.

As a result, there are entire generations today who have been educated in an attitude of intolerance of diversity. An intolerance toward those values that achieved victory in World War II but lost the war in Spain. This will make political life in Spain difficult for a while. We are, and are still trying to be, a country without memory. We haven't accepted the fact that we still need to mourn.

What do you mean?

In 1967, a couple of German psychoanalysts, Alexander and Margarete Mitscherlich, published *The Inability to Mourn*, which proposed a new way of looking at the Germans' guilt in relation to National Socialism. What the authors were referring to, however, was not the Germans' inability to mourn their victims, including the Jews, but their inability to mourn the loss of the Führer: the loss of the beloved and admired paternal authority of the criminal Nazi state. Properly mourning that loss, they argued, would be the only way to dissolve the dependency on the Führer. Around that same time, the German Right (the CDU and CSU) were working to emphasize the achievements of the country's economic miracle and arrogantly rejected any reflection on the Nazi past. Franz Josef Strauss, the president of Bavaria, used to say that when a country achieves such economic success, it has the right not to remain stuck in Auschwitz. Not long after that, this position was abandoned for its opposite. Anyone who visits Berlin today will see how the years 1930–45 are fully present throughout the city. Spain—or, rather, the Spanish Right—has not followed in the footsteps of their German counterparts. So, yes, we are still different.

8

José Antonio Zarzalejos

"We Should Be Striving toward
Restorative Justice"

"I live in a kind of no man's land," José Antonio Zarzalejos told me when we spoke in the spring of 2020. "In this
country, ideological alignments are tribal in nature. You're
a member of one group or another because it provides protection. If you're not, you end up in the line of fire. And
that's where I have been for a long time now. For the Right,
I am a fifth columnist. For the Left, I am a false moderate.
I get pummeled from both sides—but I couldn't care less."

Zarzalejos is a prominent political journalist who iden-
tifies as a conservative liberal and a Monarchist, but some
of his staunchest detractors are from the same right-wing
circles in which he grew up and spent his entire career. On
the morning after Spain's general elections of November
10, 2019, Zarzalejos was walking through Madrid, where
he's lived for over twenty years, when he was recognized
and cussed out by a stranger. "Zarzalejos!" the man yelled;

"You bastard! Dirty Red! Traitor! *¡Viva España!*" "That citizen," Zarzalejos wrote in his newspaper column the next day, "was surely one of the 3,640,063 who last Sunday voted for Vox," the Far-Right party whose support has ballooned since late 2018.

José Antonio Zarzalejos Nieto was born in 1954 as the second of five children into a conservative family that had moved to the Basque Country from Madrid a couple of years before. His paternal grandmother was a schoolteacher from San Sebastián who spoke Basque. His father, whom his son has described as a "great jurist" and "a good and upright man," was a career prosecutor in the Francoist judiciary who during the Transition worked for the Ministry of the Interior and served for a year as provincial governor of Vizcaya. Six years later, in 1982, Zarzalejos Sr. was appointed prosecutor at Spain's Supreme Court.

Today, the Zarzalejos family continues in the ranks of the country's conservative elite. José Antonio's younger brother, Javier, is a lawyer and government official who has occupied leading positions in the Partido Popular and its think tank, FAES, and is currently a member of European Parliament for the PP; his older sister, Charo, who also holds a law degree, is a well-known journalist. José Antonio grew up in Bilbao. Following in the family tradition, he went to law school, although he only worked as a lawyer until 1989, when the world of journalism beckoned. After his career change, he quickly rose to management, serving first as editor of the conservative daily *El Correo* in Bilbao—where he regularly received death threats from the terrorist organization ETA and was forced to use bodyguards—and then as editor in Madrid of *ABC*, a Monarchist fixture in

Spain's right-wing media landscape. His refusal to toe the government's line on the terrorist attacks of March 2004—which the Partido Popular insisted were perpetrated by ETA rather than by jihadists—caused a rift that eventually led to his dismissal in 2008. Since then, he's worked as a consultant, commentator, and columnist, most frequently for the online daily *El Confidencial*. He is the author of multiple books, including *Mañana será tarde* (2015; Tomorrow will be too late), *La destitución: Historia de un periodismo imposible* (2010; The destitution: History of an impossible journalism), *Contra la secesión vasca* (2005; Against the Basque secession), and *La sonrisa de Julia Roberts: Zapatero y su época* (2006; Julia Roberts' smile: Zapatero and his times).

We spoke in late May 2020, as Madrid was in the grip of the first wave of the COVID pandemic. Zarzalejos has been a vocal critic of the progressive government's handling of the health crisis. He routinely dismisses Unidas Podemos, the Socialists' junior coalition partner, as "the Paleolithic Left."

———————

Where were you when Franco died?

I was twenty-one years old and had just started my fourth year as a law student at Deusto University in Bilbao. My family on my mother's side is Monarchist. My father's family was more freethinking, but split by the Civil War, mostly because of where people happened to be when it broke out. I was quite the rebel, very critical of Franco. His regime may have made sense at one point, I thought, but he should have returned the country to democracy by 1950 at the latest.

How did you experience the exhumation in October 2019?

Its emotional significance, for me, was nil. I saw it as part of a purely propagandistic battle. The Socialist government was in desperate need of a narrative and grabbed on to Franco's grave. But it didn't work. The entire exhumation hardly caused any political tension at all. Although it happened shortly before the general elections of November 2019, polls show that its impact on those elections was negligible—especially compared to the events in Catalonia. For me, the whole exhumation and reburial seemed entirely disconnected from my life.

How are things now, seven months later?

No one talks about the Valley of the Fallen and no one bothers to visit Franco's new grave at Mingorrubio. You see, it is not an issue that Spanish society cares about. It didn't last year, and it certainly does not now. Francoism is no longer a factor in Spanish politics, either in terms of ideological identification or as a driver of the vote.

Are you really claiming that Francoism has disappeared from the political debate?

Of course, there's still a debate in Spain about Francoism. But it's a debate fueled solely, and deliberately, by the Left. The Spanish Left, you see, has very few things left to fight for. Spain, at this point, is a non-confessional country. A country where even right-wing governments defend the right to a legal abortion. A country that has legalized gay marriage and where many regional governments have included gender change in their universal healthcare package. A country whose constitutional rights and liberties are on par with those of Italy, France, or Germany. A country that is not only fully free and democratic, but whose state structure is extraordinarily decentralized, in a way that goes beyond Italy's regional organization and is not quite a federation like Germany, but that acknowledges the existence of nationalities within the Spanish nation. Finally, there is an important demographic data point: Spaniards' average age is less than fifty. More than half of the Spanish population alive today—including the generations and political leaders that now call themselves anti-Francoist—never experienced Francoism in person. Given all that, does it make sense to claim that Spain is still weighed down by remnants of Francoism? From where I am sitting, the answer to that question is a full-throated *no*. I don't believe there is any legacy of Francoism left at all.

Isn't Vox, the new Far-Right party, a Francoist holdover, or even a rebirth?

Not at all. Vox is the Spanish branch of the Far-Right European populisms that we've seen appear in other countries as well. True, compared to those other parties, Vox does have an idiosyncrasy that's clearly Hispanic: it's a confessional party. Its leaders may not be very religious, but the party has adopted religion as a mark of its identity. But that doesn't make it Francoist. If anything, it represents a reactive Spain that goes back all the way to the nineteenth century.

How about the monarchy?

It's true that Juan Carlos I de Borbón was designated as Franco's successor in 1969, as King, with all the powers that Franco had. But he rescinded all those powers in the 1978 Constitution. Not to mention that Juan Carlos hasn't been Spain's king now for six years.

I want to be sure I understand what you're saying. When you state that there is no Francoist legacy to speak of, does that mean that Spain has managed to come to terms with the legacies of the Civil War?

That is a different question. I actually think that what passes for a debate about Francoism is really, at bottom, a debate about the Civil War, which does still weigh on the country. The war was an exceptional event, incomparable even to what happened in Germany during Nazism or in Italy during fascism. People killed and were killed on both sides, Spaniards killing other Spaniards. The memory of the war still looms large in many families. The wounds are still there. What we need to do is work to heal those wounds through justice—but sensibly, striving for reconciliation, not by pitting people against each other. What we need is a collective catharsis.

You mentioned family memories. How has the war affected yours?

Two brothers of my paternal grandfather were among the thousands of prisoners who were executed by the Republican authorities at Paracuellos del Jarama in November and December of 1936. After the war, both my grandfather and my father tried to recover their remains to give them proper burial. They couldn't. Still, I never heard my father or grandfather utter a single world of resentment or ill will.

Resentment or ill will toward whom?

Toward those who killed my great-uncles. One was a lawyer and the other one a priest. I'm only bringing this up to point out that all Spanish families are marked by the war in one way or another. But if you mention this story to my children, who are thirty-one, thirty-five, and thirty-nine, they'll think you're coming from another galaxy. They don't get it at all.

As a commentator on current events, you have been critical of many aspects of Spain's democracy. In some cases, it seems to me, your point of view overlaps with that of the Left—for example, when you criticize political corruption, or the lack of independence of the press due to what you call the "promiscuity" between the media and the political and economic powers. But while the Left traces those problems back to the Francoist period and an imperfect Transition, for you their origin lies elsewhere.

It is true that some aspects of Spanish democracy are quite dysfunctional. Political corruption is a case in point. But that corruption has nothing whatsoever to do with Francoism— for one thing, because it thrives in political parties, which did not exist under Franco, and for another because it exists across the board, whether it's in the Partido Popular, the Socialist Party, or the nationalist parties in Catalonia. Its root causes are institutional inbreeding, a lack of transparency in parties' operations, and a very deficient party finance system. Plus, other Southern European countries, like Italy or France, are plagued with corruption, too.

Spain is not that different, in other words.

One obvious difference, perhaps, is that Spain doesn't exactly have a long democratic tradition. We did not experience the large democratic leaps forward that other Western European democracies experienced after 1945. This helps explain, I think, why it is difficult for us to denounce corruption, and why it has proven such a difficult problem for political parties to deal with. In Spain, for example, no one ever resigns. Politicians are not held accountable like they are in the English-speaking world, or in Germany and the Netherlands.

Another potential overlap with the Left, I feel, is your critical view of the judiciary. You've openly disagreed with some of the Supreme Court's decisions, for instance.

To be sure, there are some aspects of the judiciary that could be improved—for example, the mechanisms by which judges are selected and promoted. But overall my image of the Spanish courts is very positive. Don't forget that Spain is part of the European Convention on Human Rights, which means that it's subject to the jurisdiction of the European Court of Human Rights in Strasbourg. Similarly, all Spanish courts are subject to the European Court of Justice in Luxemburg. Our judiciary has fully internalized international law.

So those overlaps between your criticisms and those formulated by the Left are less significant than they seem.

You must understand that my critical take is rooted in a philosophical position. I am a fervent follower of Hannah Arendt. One of the lessons I took from Arendt when I was very young, and have consistently lived by since then, is that any analytical view of reality must be hostile. When I engage in a political or social analysis I do so not from a position of complacency but of intellectual hostility. This principle protects me against the temptation of facile, undocumented critique but also of any facile, undocumented praise.

If Francoism is not a root cause of Spain's challenges, where, in your view, did things go wrong?

I have a clear answer to that question. If there is a single watershed moment in the history of Spanish democracy, it's the tragedy of March 11, 2004, when Spain became the target of the most serious terrorist attack on European soil in recent history, causing 192 dead. To make things worse, the bombings happened three days before the general elections. At that point, the Partido Popular committed a grave mistake by insisting that the attack had been carried out by ETA and not by jihadists, as the Left maintained. When, three days later, the elections were unexpectedly won by the Socialist candidate, José Luis Rodríguez Zapatero, ending eight years of conservative rule, the Partido Popular launched a grave accusation. They claimed that Zapatero's election was illegitimate because the Left had taken to the streets on the day before the elections, on what should have been a day of reflection, and mounted a campaign of agitation and propaganda.

As editor of the conservative daily ABC, *you disagreed sharply with the PP's handling of the attack and its aftermath. Your position was seen as a betrayal. At the time, your brother was the general secretary of the Prime Minister, José María Aznar.*

My position on the attack ended up costing me my job. But I still think the PP committed an egregious error of judgment. The truth is that I had doubts from the beginning. I came from Bilbao, where I'd been a newspaper editor as well. I knew ETA very well. I told Aznar that same day: "President, this isn't ETA." "Why not?" he asked. "Because ETA does not commit suicide," I told him, "and ETA attacks civil guards, politicians, and the like." "But in 1987 it placed a bomb at the Hípercor shopping center!" he replied. "Yes," I said, "but they paid a heavy price for that and it ended up splitting the organization." Still, Aznar insisted, although the facts were absolutely clear: it was a jihadist attack.

And yet in the months and years following, the Right would continue to sew doubts about those facts and to insist that Zapatero's government was illegitimate.

Exactly. And the Left came up with an answer: historical memory. That is to say, the Socialist Party embraced a revisionist take on the Transition. And that's when things started going wrong.

Zapatero's willingness to revisit the Transition marked a break with the line held by Felipe González, his predecessor at the head of the Socialist Party, who was Prime Minister from 1982 until 1996.

I'm going to tell you something that may surprise you. At this point in my life, I have a very good relationship with Felipe González. Just like I had a great friendship with Alfredo Pérez Rubalcaba, who succeeded Zapatero as leader of the Socialist Party. And these friendships are compatible with the fact that I have a good relationship with José María Aznar as well. But if I am honest, I find that I am much closer, at this moment in time, to González's theses than to Aznar's.

I gather you have less admiration for Zapatero.

The moment when Zapatero jumps on the bandwagon of historical memory as a reply to the Right's attempt to delegitimize his government is the moment that everything goes south.

Because the Right digs in its heels as well.

It does. The Right, at that point, could have made a clean break and defused the entire debate. The Partido Popular could have said: "We condemn the excesses of Francoism. We agree that the Valley of the Fallen should not be a grand mausoleum for the dictator. When it comes to Francoism, we want to be on the right side of history." That's what the Right should have said at that point. But it didn't.

Hence the political mess the country is in now.

We're in a constitutional crisis, in part because the communication between the Left and the Right has become all but impossible.

I have an issue with this narrative. You make it seem as if Zapatero's embrace of the cause of historical memory, which would result in the Law of Historical Memory adopted in 2007, was a mere political response to the accusations of the Right after the 2004 elections. But by the time Zapatero was elected, a growing part of civil society had been demanding for several years already that the Spanish state intervene— for example, in relation to exhuming mass graves or dealing with the continued public presence of Francoist symbols, statues, and street names. Zapatero did not invent the memory movement, its demands for justice, or its critical view of the Transition.

That's true. But the concept of historical memory is an oxymoron. Moreover, the whole notion of memory goes against the pact of the Transition as embodied in the 1978 Constitution, which is a pact of forgetting, just like the amnesty law of 1977. Also, if we want to remember the past under the banner of historical memory, why should we stop at Francoism? Then let's go back to 1931, when the Second Republic was proclaimed—as a result of *municipal* elections, mind you. The Second Republic came about thanks to a takeover that was practically revolutionary, however peaceful it may have been. In democratic terms, the whole episode was highly questionable. All this to say that, rather than historical memory, what we should be striving toward in Spain today is restorative justice.

José Antonio Zarzalejos

But hasn't the demand for justice, including restorative justice, precisely been one of the key demands of the memory movement for the past twenty years?

Not necessarily. The demand for historical memory as formulated so far has a restorative element, but only for some Spaniards. What I am saying is that we also need reparations for the others. Restorative justice, I think, is more integrative. Let me explain. Is it reasonable and just that the mass graves be located and exhumed? Yes, of course. But are there only graves of the victims of the Francoist forces? Or also of those killed by the Republicans? My question is: where are my father's uncles?

Is it important to you to know where they are?

Personally, I am not interested at all in that question. My grandfather cared, because they were his brothers. My father cared a bit less. I don't really care at all. Still, from a logical point of view, citizens have the right to demand that the democratic state work to exhume the graves, and that it implement reparations for anyone who lost their father, mother, brothers or sisters, and so forth. Or anyone whose property was expropriated or destroyed. And those reparations should be arbitrated by a good juridical system, with full legal protections for everyone involved.

What institution do you see taking on such a task? Would it have to be created, along the lines of the truth commission that's been mentioned in electoral programs? I'd say the Spanish courts have so far shown themselves quite incapable of assuming any role at all in terms of transitional justice, starting with the Supreme Court, which, in its sentence exonerating Judge Garzón, closed all doors to any judicial solution for the victims of the Franco regime.

On that last point I disagree. When the Supreme Court exonerated Garzón of the charges that were brought after he opened an investigation of the so-called crimes of Francoism, the sentence stated that no one can be held accountable before a *criminal* court for acts committed during the war and the dictatorship. Not only because any of those crimes would have prescribed but also because of the amnesty law. Still, the sentence leaves room for civil or administrative claims. Also, the exhumations of mass graves are by now overseen by local judicial authorities. In other words, I do see a central role for the judiciary in this process.

That would first require a different kind of legislation. How should the memory law be changed, in your view?

It should be transformed into a universal law of reparation for all Spaniards. And yes, any symbol in the country's public spaces that rekindles the conflicts of the civil war should be neutralized. We should not have streets named after anyone involved in the war. Our public spaces should connote reconciliation, honoring names that bring us together instead of tearing us apart. But that work has never been seriously taken on because there is no political will. If there were political will, mechanisms would be found to get it done. That's how it always works in a democracy. In the same way that it would only be proper in a democracy for the courts to oversee the process of reparations if such a law were adopted.

Would the courts in their current composition be able or willing to take that on? Given the political profile of the judiciary, I'd have my doubts—and I'm sure I'm not the only one.

Of course they'd be able to. You know, one of the most unfair stigmas that the Spanish judiciary suffers is that it would be ultraconservative. That's just not true at all. From the General Council of the Judiciary to the Supreme Court and the Constitutional Court, there is an extraordinary variety of political profiles, both progressive and conservative. The Spanish justice system is no different from those in other European countries. Just look at the Supreme Court's verdict that found some political leaders from Catalonia guilty of sedition, in October 2019. More than a third of its 433 pages are dedicated to demonstrating that the rights of the accused were fully respected, not only by Spanish standards but by the doctrine of the Human Rights Court in Strasbourg! The sentence is now being appealed at the Constitutional Court, after which it is appealable in Strasbourg. And whatever the European court decides will carry the day. It can't really get any better than that from a democratic standpoint. Similarly, we have *habeas corpus*; Spain's law to protect women and punish gender violence is exemplary from a European standpoint, and so forth. I honestly find it hard to find flaws when it comes to the caliber of Spain's democracy.

Not one?

Come to think of it, there is one—and if it were up to me, it would be solved as soon as possible. I'm talking about the privileged treatment of the Catholic Church by the Spanish state. I grew up Catholic, although I don't practice. But I do not understand why it's the state's job to collect money for the Church through income tax declarations. Nor do I understand why all the governments we've had, not just from the Right but from the Left, from González through Zapatero and now Sánchez, have never revised Spain's agreements with the Vatican. Those date from 1979!

Well, there you have it. Some would say that treatment of the Church is precisely one of the legacies of Francoism that persist in Spain today.

I grant you that. But you know what? If at this moment the Prime Minister would say, "Folks, one of the goals of this government is to revise the 1979 agreement with the Vatican," it would not be a big deal. Ninety percent of Spaniards would accept it.

But the Catholic hierarchy not so much.

Part of the hierarchy would protest, sure. But only a part. Because it, too, has seen a generational turnover. We now have bishops in their forties.

You mentioned you grew up Catholic. Anyone who reads your biography will realize you've been shaped by your upbringing. What portion of your political views, or your view on Spanish history, can be traced back to your genealogy? Could you have grown up to be a Communist or, I don't know, a member of the izquierda abertzale, *a left-wing proponent of Basque independence?*

No, I don't think so. [*Laughter.*] Look, I don't believe in determinism. But we are all shaped by our circumstances. From a young age, and within the environment of my up-bringing, I have adhered to both rational analysis and empathy. As a result of my analysis, I empathize with some elements from my environment and not with others. In other words, I am a product of my environment and family, but I am also the product of my own critical autonomy, driven by an intellectual effort that has brought me close to people with very different beliefs than mine, and to formative readings by a variety of authors, some of whom are close to my family context while others are at the opposite end.

In a political context as polarized as Spain's, I imagine that puts you in a complicated position.

When the Civil War broke out, Salvador de Madariaga, a great intellectual and federalist, refused to take sides. He said he represented the "third Spain." My case is the same. When I'm asked who my political point of reference in Spain might be, I can't come up with anyone. Outside of Spain, it's Angela Merkel, the German chancellor. I like how she deals with immigration issues. I like her position on Germany's terrible Nazi past. I admire how brutally critical she can be of her own country, and the way she refuses to work with the Far Right as well as the Far Left, sticking to social democracy in a broad coalition government. Not to mention her integrity.

Your intellectual point of reference, you mentioned earlier, is also German: Hannah Arendt. Do you have one within Spain?

Miguel de Unamuno.

I can see that. Like you, he was a Basque from Bilbao who liked to situate himself in no man's land.

Unamuno was a man full of contradictions, anxieties, and perplexities. But that's how one must live. Living in the present means allowing yourself to be surprised.

9

Politics and the
Territorial Challenge

"Why is it so hard for the Partido Popular to condemn Franco-ism?" a reporter from *La voz de Galicia* asked Jaime Mayor Oreja in 2007. "That's because Francoism is part of Spanish history," the then fifty-six-year-old Mayor Oreja replied. "How am I going to condemn something that undoubtedly represented a very broad sector of Spaniards?" An interesting exchange followed:

REPORTER: By that same logic, you wouldn't condemn Nazism or Stalinism either, because they were supported by many German and Soviet citizens.

JAIME MAYOR OREJA: In the [Civil] War there were two sides, and in Nazism only one.

R: During Francoism, there was only one side that imposed repression.

JMO: No, there were two, because Francoism was the result of a Civil War in which there were two sides. It's not the same as the Nazi regime, in which there was only one perpetrator.

R: So . . . you don't think it's pertinent to condemn Francoism?

JMO: No, I don't, for many reasons. Why would I condemn Francoism when there were many families who experienced it as natural and normal? In my region, the Basque country . . ., the war was much worse than Francoism. . . . Let's leave the analysis of Francoism to the historians. (Clemente 2007)

By 2007, Mayor Oreja had had a distinguished political career. A co-founder of the conservative Partido Popular (PP), he served as a deputy in the Spanish and Basque parliaments, minister of the interior, and a member of European Parliament. In that last role, he'd spoken in July 2006 on behalf of his party in reaction to the request from two hundred deputies to condemn the Franco dictatorship on the seventieth anniversary of the military coup that unleashed the war in Spain. Mayor Oreja forcefully rejected the idea of a condemnation. Instead, he proposed to celebrate what he called "reconciliation" and "harmony." "There are many Spaniards who think, like me, that trying to push for a second Transition today is a historical error," he said, "as if the first Transition had turned old and obsolete. It's a historical error unilaterally to break with the essence of our Constitution" (Reyes Guzmán 2012, 12:25–14:40).

Mayor Oreja's position—a staunch defense of the Transition and a refusal to say anything negative of the dictatorship—was symptomatic. His party, the PP, seems constitutionally incapable of distancing itself from

Francoism and the ideological currents from which it sprung. "The Spanish Right has been unable to build an alternative political genealogy, one that connects with other branches of conservatism," the historian Jaume Claret told me. "And given what Ivan Krastev and Stephen Holmes are calling an 'outbreak of reactionary nativism' worldwide, the Right is retreating into familiar territory—a terrain that can no longer be called Francoism per se, but that's chock full of holdovers from it."

In 1976, the PP was founded as Alianza Popular by Manuel Fraga, who until 1969 served in Franco's cabinet as minister of information and tourism. As recently as 2018, the party refused to support a parliamentary motion condemning the Franco dictatorship "and any act extolling it" (Monforte Jaén 2018). Before the vote, the PP had proposed an amendment condemning any foundation or association "that extols or glorifies Nazism, fascism, Communism, and all the populist ideologies that incite conflict among citizens"—an obvious attempt to force the hand of the parliamentary Left, in particular Podemos. Predictably, the amendment was rejected, and the PP deputies voted against the original motion.

The one occasion on which the PP came closest to denouncing the dictatorship occurred in 2002, when the party joined a parliamentary majority in condemning the 1936 coup. Since then, the PP has stubbornly abstained from explicit critiques of the Franco regime. In 2003, it refused to join in a tribute to the victims of Francoism; in 2007, it voted against the Law of Historical Memory; in 2013, it rejected turning July 18 into a Day of Condemnation of the Dictatorship; in 2015, it voted against the removal of

Francoist symbols and street names and against the extradi-
tion to Argentina of former Francoist ministers (Monforte
Jaén 2018). In 2019, the newly installed PP government in
Madrid decided to dismantle a monument displaying thousands of names of victims of the dictatorship that the previous administration had begun constructing. If the party's
position has evolved in any way, it seems, it has been toward retrenchment. In our interview, Claret, the historian,
agreed. "The politicians who served as the executors of the
dictatorship, so to speak, tried hard to steer clear of any
direct link to it. Instead, they spoke of the need to avoid
opening old wounds. But what started out as a defensive
attitude has by now turned into more combative and ideological positions. This has gone hand in hand with the rise
of historical revisionism."

Meanwhile, the PP's reactions to the demands of the
memory movement have been awkward if not outright
dismissive. The party's current leader, Pablo Casado, went
out of his way to offend the victims' associations when, as
a rising young deputy, he gave a speech at the 2009 party
congress in which he suggested that those looking for the
remains of their loved ones were stuck in the past. "I am
convinced," he said, "that the immense majority of young
people identify with the Partido Popular, even though they
don't know it yet. In the twenty-first century, there is no
way that being a leftist is fashionable. Leftists are retrograde.
They won't stop talking about grandpa's war, about the
mass grave of I-don't-know-who, about historical memory"
(Catalán 2015). Rafael Hernando, then the PP's spokesper-
son in Parliament, said in 2013 that "some of the victims
of Francoism only remember their parents when there are

subsidies available to help find them" (Junquera 2013). Three
years later, in a television interview with Jordi Évole in the
popular weekly documentary program *Salvados*, then prime
minister Rajoy of the PP was caught in a painful exchange.
"You often invoke common sense," Évole told Rajoy. ". . .
But do you think it makes sense that, in 2016, thousands of
Spaniards still don't know where their grandparents are buried?" Rajoy's reply illustrated how far the memory movement had been able to move the needle of public opinion—
and how little the PP had been able to move along with it:

RAJOY: I would like it if everyone knew where their grandparents are buried, but I am not sure that what you say is
true, or that the government can do anything about it.

ÉVOLE: Come on, Mr. Rajoy, what I just said *is* true.

RAJOY: Yes, there are evidently many people who do
not know, of course. But after what happened in Spain
years ago, the most common-sensical thing to do, it seems
to me, is to try for those kinds of things to not happen
again, and to not be returning to the past time and time
again. (LaSexta 2016a)

As cringe-inducing as these answers were, the truth is
that the PP's difficulty with publicly distancing itself from
the dictatorship—or simply acknowledging that the Transition left important business unfinished—is not the most
problematic legacy of Francoism in Spanish politics today.
This, at least, is the view of José Luis Villacañas, a professor
of philosophy at the Universidad Complutense in Madrid.
Where Francoism survives most clearly, he told me, is not
in symbolic acknowledgments or their absence, but in the

very conception of what it means to practice democratic politics. This conception manifests in a "mentality among the central elites" that can be described in precise detail.

When it comes to managing problems that affect their interests, Villacañas said, the elites "simply do not accept political mediation." Worse, they tend to "treat different political interests as if they were *enemy* interests." Politics, in other words, is understood not as negotiation but as outright war. "'Any political position that I do not understand or share,' Spanish politicians tell themselves, 'has to be defeated, conquered—and, if at all possible, neutralized and punished,'" Villacañas said. This legacy has little to do with sociological Francoism, he pointed out. Sociologically speaking, in fact, "Francoism was apolitical": the bulk of the population "was encouraged to stay out of politics altogether." The elites, on the other hand, were conditioned by the dictatorship to "instrumentalize the apparatus of the state to target political interests and ideas that were different from their own—and to destroy them to the point of annihilation." The persistence of this attitude until decades after Franco's death goes a long way to explaining the dysfunctions of party politics in Spain today. Spanish elites, in fact, have had tremendous trouble accepting basic principles, Villacañas said. "There is a real deficit when it comes to understanding the political structures of democracy, whether it's the Parliament, the function of critique, the true meaning of the separation of powers, a democratic understanding of the role and functioning of a political party, or the conception of public life."

As others have pointed out, many of the phenomena that we can identify as legacies of Francoism existed prior to Franco's rise to power. "In many ways, for example," Villacañas told me, "Franco's regime realized the aspirations of the dictatorship of Miguel Primo de Rivera," who ruled the country from 1923 until 1930. His ascent to power served to quell the crisis of the monarchy, half a century after its restoration following a brief Republican interval. What made the Franco regime so decisive, however, was its ability to incorporate, crystallize, and perpetuate the attitudes, practices, and aspirations of previous periods. Such was its ability, in fact, that those crystallized attitudes, practices, and aspirations survive in Spanish politics to this day. "There is not a single problem in our democracy today," Villacañas said, "whose genealogy is not rooted in this Francoist crystallization, however much we might trace its origin to those more archaic strata."

Pablo Sánchez León, a historian, agreed with Villacañas: while Francoism drew on existing traditions of conservative thought, it transformed those traditions in a decisive way. "I don't think that the problems Spain faces today go much further back than Francoism. To assume that they do opens the door to the facile stereotype of Spain's eternal ills." For Sánchez León, it was under Francoism that Spain underwent the social and economic transformations that help explain the country's problems in the post-Franco period. The key, he explains, was the fact that the country's rapid urbanization and industrialization of the 1950s and '60s was not joined by any change in political regime. "It's in the gap that resulted that sociological Francoism was forged," he told me. On the one hand, civil society was shaped by market relations and accompanying values like consumption, mesocracy, and individualism. On the other, the political order remained essentially anti-civic, ruled by a despotic regime that discouraged autonomous citizen participation. "This opened up a space for informal relations in which citizens promoted their own interests but never in the service of mobilization, let alone protest." This modus operandi not only survived into the democratic period but became more prevalent. According to Sánchez León, it is this dynamic that explains the pervasiveness of political and corporate corruption. "It's true that the globalization of finance has led to corruption in many places. Still, in Spain it takes on a very specific set of features rooted in the country's entire political culture, whether we're talking about parties in government or in the opposition."

Sebastián Martín, who teaches legal history at the University of Sevilla, also pointed to the nineteenth-century origins of Francoism as a political identity when I spoke with him in late 2019. The central elements of this identity, he argued, are less than compatible with the logic of a modern constitutional democracy. He went on to provide an exhaustive inventory of features. These include "a hierarchical conception of society" and "a uniform, imperial understanding of the nation, identified culturally with the Catholic faith." In this form of political culture, certain institutions, like the monarchy, are granted a preconstitutional status, not subject to collective consent. Public life should steer clear of politics altogether (as in the motto "do like me, don't get mixed up in politics"). In addition, major disagreements are preferably resolved "through the imposition of will: the authoritarian solution of the 'iron hand.'"

Translated into everyday political practice, Martín explained, these ideas prompt repressive rather than democratic solutions to conflicts. They also tend to privilege politics as expressed through institutions rather than through popular participation, and as embodied in large, official forms of consensus next to which any form of disagreement can be dismissed as "radical" or "anti-system." Historian Luis de Guezala agreed. "As under Francoism, political legitimacy is seen to reside in the law rather than in the will of the people." This tendency has in fact increased in recent years, he added. "Since Felipe VI ascended to the throne in 2014, the monarchy and the national government have turned into unabashed defenders of this theory."

The Francoist influence in Spanish political culture is further noticeable in "a notorious inclination to treat public institutions as if they are private property," Martín said, along with the explicit exercise of personal power: "a capacity for decision-making that goes beyond all the normative constrictions of the rule of law, tends to devolve into measures taken for the politician's personal benefit, and yet, at the same time, protects the behavior of the power holders with a cloak of impunity." In this political culture, elites are bound together by a deep-seated solidarity that "links success in business and the accumulation of wealth with enjoying the protection and special treatment of public institutions," in practice turning the administration, at all levels of government, into instruments to benefit corporations. All of this, finally, translates into a "systemic corruption, through the bribing of any regulators and political representatives in charge of making decisions about public contracts, service contracts or, in the context of the dictatorship, monopolies and tariffs."

These Francoist traits of Spanish political culture are not merely operative on the right side of the spectrum, Martín pointed out. The reactions to the Catalan crisis in 2017—from the slogan *¡A por ellos!* (*Let's go get them!*) brandished by the national police as they marched toward Catalonia to the media coverage of the conflict—show these traits are also shared by groups and parties that identify as leftist. Other Francoist holdovers that have affected the political spectrum more broadly include the state's law-and-order response to the social protests in the wake of the Great Recession, or the high levels of political corruption that seem to be endemic to all levels of administration.

For the political scientist Guillermo Fernández and the historian Luis de Guezala, the traces of Francoism in Spain today are most evident in the disputes about the country's organizational makeup. "Sociological Francoism worries me most when it comes to imagining Spain's political identity and territorial structure," Fernández told me. "On the one hand, many Spaniards find it very hard to think about Spanish identity in anything but essentialist terms. On the other, there is still a strong resistance to embracing the country's multiplicity of languages and cultures as a form of wealth and, especially, as something that belongs to everyone. In the end, sociological Francoism has tended to tolerate the existence of languages like Catalan, Galician, and Basque as a lesser evil, something it has no choice but to accept, but that fortunately is limited to certain regions. In this view, the other languages of the Spanish state will always be small, regional, and subordinate to the commonly held language, Spanish." For Fernández, this lingering Francoist attitude explains why Spain's centralist political elites have been unable to "disarm" the power of peripheral nationalisms. It also explains why Spanish democracy, marked by this Francoist legacy, "has always constructed its identity and its common sense in opposition to an internal other: first the Basque independence movement and now Catalonia." For de Guezala, Francoism survives in the way Spanish constitutionalism has turned "the defense of territorial unity into its central objective—a responsibility delegated, moreover, to the armed forces."

The Valencian journalist Miquel Ramos agrees. "Through the centuries, Spain has been inhabited by many different identities, whether they were Jewish, Roma, Muslim, or immigrants" he said. "But these have never been sufficiently acknowledged. If they weren't silenced, they were considered a problem—as is the case still today with the communities that represent Spain's cultural and linguistic diversity. Ironically, it's those of us who *defend* that diversity who tend to be accused of being nationalist and exclusionary." Spain, Ramos told me, has never been uniform: "There is no single way of being Spanish, or a citizen of the Spanish state—however much the dominant Spanish nationalist narrative that's rooted in Francoism tries to deny that diversity."

Yet if the legacies of Francoism manifest themselves in dismissive or repressive attitudes toward the linguistic and cultural minorities on the periphery, Ramos's position shows that the periphery has been pushing back. As we saw in Chapters 1 and 2, Basque and Catalan politicians who favor independence have come to believe that they provide what little hope there is for democratic renewal in the Spanish state. Going by the way they operate in Madrid, one is tempted to conclude that they are right. In recent years, Basque and Catalan politicians have assumed a peculiar role in the Spanish parliament: They've become the only ones capable of naming things for what they are. Deputies like Gabriel Rufián of the Catalan Left Republicans or Oskar Matute of EH Bildu have turned their interventions into a truth-telling performance about their fellow deputies' acts of corruption, manipulation, or hypocrisy. As self-declared outsiders with no investment in Spain's national institutions, they have been relatively free from the taboos that weigh down the other deputies—and they clearly derive immense enjoyment from the ability to call a spade a spade. Still, politics *within* the autonomous communities of the Basque Country, Galicia, and Catalonia are less different than the peripheral politicians' truth-telling behavior in Madrid would seem to indicate. Once back in their own regions, the lightness that the Basques and Catalans display in the national capital disappears. At home, they, too, are tangled in intrigues, opportunism, and doublespeak. The history of the Catalan *procés*, the roadmap to independence laid out by a coalition of parties that straddles the Left-Right divide, illustrates this well.

Catalonia is one of the seventeen "autonomous communities" that make up post-Franco Spain. In the Catalan case, autonomy includes the right to its own co-official language, its own police force, and its own educational policies, although Spain's 1978 Constitution stipulates "the indissoluble unity of the Spanish Nation" and does not provide for secession or self-determination. Over the past decade and a half, what once seemed the best possible way to accommodate Spain's multinational make-up is now coming apart at the seams, pushing the country to the edge of a constitutional crisis. As the sociologist Manuel Castells, currently Spain's minister of universities, said on Catalan television in October 2019, the "problem is very simple": "Spanish legality is not recognized as such by approximately half of Catalonia's population. And up to 70 or 75 percent believe that the only way out of the problem is a vote: a peaceful, tranquil referendum" (TV3 2019, 7:55).

Madrid and Barcelona are separated by multiple barriers. Some are cultural and linguistic; others are more recent and man-made. The distance would be less significant, for example, if schoolchildren in Madrid would not just study Castilian but Catalan as well—or, for that matter, Galician or Basque. In theory, nothing would be more normal in a state like Spain, two of whose most economically advanced regions are bilingual. But in practice, nothing is farther removed from Spanish common sense. ("Why should my child learn Catalan?" my friends in Madrid and Andalusia say; "English is much more useful!") The attitude is symptomatic of the scarce acceptance among many Spaniards, including the political elites, of Spain's multinational makeup. As a result, relations between Catalans and Spaniards suffer from a chronic lack of understanding and empathy, nourished by a dearth of reliable information. In his intensive coverage of the apparently intractable conflict between Madrid and Barcelona over self-determination, the journalist Guillem Martínez has argued that, at bottom, the crisis has been a shadow play between two conservative parties desperate to maintain their grip on power: the Catalan Convergència Democràtica de Catalunya (CDC, whose later metamorphoses include PDeCat and Junts pel Sí) and the Spanish

Partido Popular (PP) (Martínez 2016). Despite their nasty public fight over Catalonia's status, at bottom they share the same economic and political interests. Their alliances with each other and with the country's corporate elite are solidified in backroom meetings and covert agreements—and rooted in the mutual awareness of each other's deep-seated corruption, most tangibly embodied in years' worth of corporate kickbacks of between 3 and 5 percent in exchange for lucrative government contracts.

The story of the recent troubles begins in 2006, when the Catalan and Spanish parliaments both approved an updated Statute of Autonomy for Catalonia. In 2010, responding to an appeal filed by the PP, Spain's Constitutional Court rejected some of the statute's key provisions. The verdict hit Catalonia like a bombshell, sparking a massive grass-roots movement in which broad sectors of civil society demanded independence. Catalonia's political class took note. Convergència—a conservative-Catholic and *catalanista* party that had never been in favor of full independence—saw a chance to reverse the steady erosion of its support. Long hegemonic in regional politics and identified with its leader Jordi Pujol (president of Catalonia from 1980 until 2003), Convergència's image was suffering from corruption scandals and the ruthless cuts it made to health care, education, and social services in the wake of the Great Recession.

In September 2012, Convergència leader Artur Mas, Catalan president since 2010, jumped on the independence bandwagon. "It is time that Catalonia exercises its right to self-determination," he said in a speech to parliament, announcing a political process (*procés* in Catalan) toward that goal. In the run-up to regional elections in 2015, Mas managed to convince several other parties, including the Republican Left (ERC), to join in an electoral coalition for independence, called Junts pel Sí (JxS, Together for Yes). The assembly-based, Far-Left Candidatura d'Unitat Popular (CUP, Candidacy for Popular Unity) pledged parliamentary support. The combined pro-independence parties won a narrow majority of seats in the Catalan parliament. And while they fell short of a majority of the popular vote, they nevertheless claimed a popular mandate to go ahead with the preparations for secession—leading up to the referendum of October 1, 2017, which took place despite the violent attempts of Catalan and Spanish police to stop it. The referendum led to a drawn-out judicial process that pushed several Catalan leaders into exile and, in October 2019, led to twelve convictions for sedition, misappropriation of funds, and civil disobedience.

For Martínez, it was all part of a pantomime that, in addition to polarizing positions throughout Spain, led the country into a massive political morass. The truth, he writes, is that the so-called *procés* has been the opposite of what it has claimed to be. Where it promised progress, it heightened stagnation. Where it invoked democracy, it promoted its erosion. The way Martínez sees it, the *procés* is an empty promise whose fulfillment is infinitely postponed. Its real purpose is the survival of an entire political class in the face of a crisis of legitimacy. The reinvention of the Catalan Right, which changed its name to Partit Demòcrata Europeu Català (Catalan European Democratic Party, PDeCat) after joining the pro-independence movement, is purely rhetorical. The politicians spearheading the *procés* have substituted concepts endowed with some legal or historical reality—"referendum," for example—with others that resemble it but don't exist legally, such as "consultation." The Catalan political class, in other words, has been operating like salesmen peddling branded sneakers whose logos, upon closer inspection, say "Niki" or "Now Balance."

This does not mean that the aspirations to statehood are misplaced. Martínez, like many Catalans and some Spaniards, believes that Catalonia exists as a nation with its own history and identity. In his 2016 book *La gran ilusión*, he points to the region's long history of proto-democratic experiences and experiments, ranging from the Consell de Cent (Council of 100) that governed Barcelona from the thirteenth to the eighteenth centuries to the Anarchist experiments in collectivization during the first months of the Spanish Civil War—which, as Sam Dolgoff writes, "came closer to realizing the ideal of the free stateless society on a vast scale than any other revolution in history" (Dolgoff 1974, 5). The great Catalan thinker Francesc Pi i Margall (1824–1901), Martínez tells us, proposed an idea of the state "understood as a federation of [sovereign] individuals who mutually agree on their union." His brand of republicanism, "federal and libertarian" in character, featured "advanced social and economic ideas, such as an early concept of the welfare state; a commitment to the cooperative as a means to establish collective ownership of the means of production; abolition of slavery; and a reasoned and peaceful solution to Spanish imperialism in America and Asia" (2016, 40–41).

Despite the posturing of its political class, then, Martínez maintains that the Catalan nation is real. In fact, he suggests, it may well be more real than Spain, which has been based less on a shared past and future aspirations than on a forcibly imposed hierarchy and, above all, systematic exclusion of the cultural other. At the end of the fifteenth century, Martínez writes, the newly created Spanish state "seems to have understood that its political project was to penalize difference" (2016, 26). This was also the project of the Francoist state. The responses from Madrid to the Catalan independence movement over the past decade have only served to confirm this impression.

FURTHER READING

Spain's territorial disputes over the past half century have sparked a massive bibliography in Spanish, English, and other languages, in various disciplines. For a general, journalistic introduction to the recent growth of the Catalan independence movement, see Minder (2017); for a comparative approach from a historian's point of view, see Elliott (2018). For an excellent critical take on Spanish nationalism, also by an historian, see Núñez Seixas (2018), in Spanish or, for a shorter, English version, Núñez Seixas (2020). See also Hierro (2020). Gabilondo (2019a) approaches questions of Spanish nationalism and the state in an original and enlightening way through literature and cultural theory. For a useful English-language overview of the disputes around Spanish nationhood that preceded the escalation of the Catalan conflict, see Humlebæk (2015).

10

Enric Juliana

*"We Can't Call Everything
We Don't Like Francoist"*

Enric Juliana was eighteen when Franco died. "My memory
of that moment illustrates its profound double-sidedness,"
he told me. "When I came down that morning, my father
said: 'He's dead.' He was tense, clearly out of sorts, as if the
order of things had come undone. My dad, you see, was
a young child when the Civil War broke out. He grew up
in an industrial neighborhood in Badalona, near Barcelona.
When he was six, he witnessed how anarchists burned down
the church where he'd received his first communion. That
terrified him. The town was also a frequent bombing target
for the Italian air force, which killed one of his childhood
friends. Growing up with that kind of trauma, my father
had become psychologically invested in the idea of order.
So, naturally, Franco's death left him disoriented. But that
wasn't my case. I felt it was the beginning of something
new and exciting, although I had no idea of what. That

same afternoon I got together with friends to celebrate. We toasted with champagne."

Born in Badalona in 1957, Enric Juliana is the associate editor and Madrid correspondent at *La Vanguardia*, Catalonia's newspaper of record and one of Spain's three most-read generalist dailies. Owned by the Count of Godó, a prominent aristocrat and businessman, the paper holds to a conservative editorial line and has been close to the pro-Catalan Right since the Transition. In recent years, thanks in large part to the success of its website, which runs stories in both Spanish and Catalan, its audience across Spain has increased significantly.

Juliana cuts an unusual figure in Madrid's media landscape. More well-read—and better dressed—than most of his colleagues, he projects an image of sophistication and intellectual curiosity. His columns, in which he likes to connect day-to-day developments with larger historical trends, have a certain literary flair. In his frequent TV appearances, he analyzes Spanish politics in a heavy Catalan accent with the amused fascination of an outsider. One gets the impression he'd be equally comfortable at a dinner party with the nobleman who publishes his paper as discussing Lenin over late-night drinks in a Barcelona bar. His grandfathers baked bread and worked metal; his father worked as an accountant at a factory and, after he was laid off, in a bakery. In his youth, Juliana joined the PSUC, the Catalan branch of the then-clandestine Communist Party. His position today can be described as moderate liberal in the European sense. His years as *La Vanguardia*'s correspondent in Italy have left him with an abiding love of that country, and he's long had a weak spot for Antonio Gramsci. We spoke on the telephone at the end of May 2020, after more than two months of pandemic-induced lockdown.

———————

What did you think of Franco's exhumation?

I had mixed feelings. I understood the need for it, of course. Having a mausoleum of that type in a democracy is simply unacceptable. But I didn't agree with the government's attempt to turn the event into a national catharsis—especially so close to an electoral campaign. Situating the country emotionally around Franco's dead body shortly before a general election did not get my heart racing, so to speak. In my view, it would have been preferable, and more discreet, to wait with the exhumation until right after the elections. Instead, the event turned into something of an exorcism. It was inappropriate.

Inappropriate in what way?

Politically. Because Franco is long gone. Francoism has disappeared.

Has it? Completely?

All that's left is radiation. Francoism, like all radioactive isotopes, has a very long half-life.

Does that mean you let it slowly decay on its own, or do you cover it in a thick layer of lead?

You cover it in lead, and you don't mess with it.

When Franco died, you were a member of Catalonia's Communist Party.

It was a formative experience, and I have a wonderful affective memory of those years. Being submerged in politics at a moment like that shaped who I am today. I have never seen that period as a mistake or a form of extravagance. It wasn't like I'd gone off the deep end. After all, the PSUC at that time was seen by some on the Left as a moderate party! [*Laughs.*] Although in rational terms I no longer subscribe to the ideas I had then, the lessons I learned in those years have been useful later in life. Now perhaps more than ever, because once again this country is facing a critical moment, the outcome of which is as unclear as it was to us then.

It was a different time, to be sure.

Yes, of course. Most importantly, we were still in the Cold War and the PSUC, as a party, played for the other team—although, incredibly, we fooled ourselves into thinking that we had a foot on both sides of the Iron Curtain. There certainly was an element of fantasy in that belief. I learned a lot about the sorcery that is politics. [*Laughs.*] Here's an anecdote for you. I remember that, within the party, we had small internal competitions to see which of the local party groups managed to distribute most copies of our paper, things like that—to motivate us. Now get this: at one point, the party offered as a prize a chunk of the wing of an American fighter jet shot down in Vietnam, which the

North Vietnamese had sent to the PSUC as a gift. If I remember correctly, the Sabadell group won the prize. I've
always wondered what happened to that piece of airplane.
One day I'd love to do a reportage to find out.

*A chunk of an American airplane that functions like the incorrupt
arm of Saint Theresa.*

A relic, indeed.

*I want to ask you about Spain today, about which there are two
conflicting narratives. One states that Spanish democracy may have
some challenges but that, in general terms, it is not much different
from, and certainly not worse than, those of neighboring countries
like France or Italy. The other claims that Spain's democracy is
not only seriously deficient but that most of its dysfunctions can be
traced back to the Franco period, thanks in large part to a democratic
transition that was left woefully unfinished. Where do you stand?*

Although I don't agree with those who are most critical of
the Transition, we have to accept the fact that the Spanish
dictatorship had a softer landing than most other European
dictatorships. In Portugal, the Salazar regime plummeted
to its death. In Greece, too, the dictatorship ended more
abruptly. In Spain, by contrast, the dictatorship tranquilly
shut itself down and negotiated a pact with the democratic
opposition—a negotiation in which the outgoing regime
held a clear home-field advantage.

That said, it is also true that what ended up happening
in Spain had very little to do with the Francoists' original program. The Francoists knew from the late 1960s that

Spain would have to liberalize politically. But what they envisioned was a much slower, more gradual process. A Constitution like the one that got approved in 1978 was definitely not part of their plans. Nor was the legalization of the Communist Party, or the central role that the labor unions ended up playing. Organizing the country into autonomous communities was also not something they had envisioned. Why did everything turn out so differently? Because of the political dynamics of the moment and, of course, the results of the elections. So, I don't agree with those who argue that the democratic opposition capitulated to the Franco regime. The opposition got as much out of the process it as it could at the time—to the extent, that is, that it had real roots in Spanish society.

A society profoundly marked by almost forty years of state repression.

Franco's dictatorship was ruthless. It was founded on a military victory that sought not only to defeat the enemy but to destroy him. Franco was bent on rooting out his adversaries. That explains the systematic repression and mass exile. By the 1930s, Spanish society had begun to develop a democratic awareness. Yet Franco deprogrammed it from top to bottom, wiping out that budding democratic awareness in both political and cultural terms. When democracy returns to Spain, our society is still in a deprogrammed state. In the years following, it undergoes a reprogramming process that's highly accelerated but also uneven. Between 1977 and, let's say, 1986, which is when Spain enters the European Common Market, the country sees a political liberalization that's much faster than the Francoists were willing to allow for initially. At the same time, Spanish ways of life go through profound changes as well. In a period of ten years, Spain basically turns into a post-traditional society. The Catholic Church rapidly loses all the influence it wielded under Franco. This factor is often underestimated, but it's important—and it certainly was a thorn in the side of Pope John Paul II. It helps explain, for example, why Spain today stands out when it comes to women's rights or legalizing same-sex marriage.

But the traces of the dictatorship didn't disappear overnight.

Of course they didn't. Just like the traces of Salazarism haven't disappeared in Portugal, either.

And those traces are perhaps most evident in the continuities among the political and economic elites.

Sure, but one should be careful not to confuse Francoism with what I'd call *oligarchic crystallizations*. Those happen anywhere. When Giscard d'Estaing, the former French President, was discovered to have been involved in unsavory business with diamonds in Africa, did that mean he was somehow linked to Marshall Pétain and the Vichy Regime? Of course not. He was a Republican French President. But France has its interests, its zones of influence, its economic deals.

How about the big stakeholders in the media?

In terms of media power, it's interesting to remember that the French media, with the exception of *Le Monde*, have historically been heavily influenced by the proprietors of industry. The same is true for Italy. The first publisher of *La Repubblica* was Carlo de Benedetti, who owned Olivetti. The publishers of the *Corriere della Sera* were a North-Italian business syndicate.

For the Spanish case, many have pointed out that the families that became rich and powerful under Francoism continue to make up much of the country's current elite.

Sure, but that is simply because they're the ruling classes! In Spain, as we know, there was no historical break with Francoism. But then again, in Portugal the Banco Espíritu Santo was with Salazar. Just like in Germany many of the large companies that financed Hitler's regime continue to operate.

Although some of the largest German corporations have by now been forced to pay reparations to victims of the Holocaust, something that has yet to happen in Spain.

Look, I think it's entirely legitimate that Spain continues to find out everything that happened and everyone who was involved during Francoism. But that doesn't mean we can call everything we don't like Francoist.

The continuity of family names, or what you call oligarchic crystallizations, is one thing. Another is the cultural anthropology of elite behavior. To what extent has Francoism left traces at the level of habits or tics, modes of operation or relation to each other?

Those tendencies persist to some extent. Madrid, in particular, is an intricate network of relations. But, once again, if you compare Spain with Italy, you'll see that the capitalist system there has been much more closed than here. Spain began opening itself up to foreign markets in the early 1960s. And look at the situation today. The country's print daily of reference, *El País*, is owned by foreigners. Sure, it has Spanish managers, but its financial ups and downs have left it controlled by a US investment fund. But even the original stakeholders of *El País* were people I would not characterize as members of the Francoist oligarchy.

But Jesús de Polanco, the paper's founder, was a successful businessman during the regime.

He'd done well in the textbook business. But I would not include him in the circle of powerful families.

I interrupted you. You were talking about foreign markets.

It's quite remarkable. To stay in the world of the media, the daily *El Mundo* is owned by the publisher of *Corriere della Sera*. Its owners were interested in buying a Spanish paper because they also owned Fiat, which was angry at Felipe González because he had given the Seat factory to Volkswagen, in Germany, along with the main network of automobile outlets in Spain. The Italians didn't mind losing the factory but were furious about the distribution network. And they realized it was attractive to have a newspaper in Spain dedicated to harassing González. But *El Mundo* is no exception. The television network *Telecinco* is owned by

Silvio Berlusconi. Almost half of *Antena 3* is owned by De-Agostini. Now, in Italy it'd be unthinkable that the country's second most important newspaper and some of the leading TV networks would be in Spanish hands. It'd be considered a national affront, a problem of national sovereignty. In France, the same. In Spain, it's not an issue.

You'd half expect a nationalist party like Vox to bring that up.

Ah, well, for folks in Vox the issue of sovereignty is relative. [*Laughs.*] It matters to them in some areas but less in others.

Let's move to another sphere of the state. So far, you've downplayed the continuities with Francoism. How about the judicial branch?

That is a critical point, I think. Because the Transition was the result of a negotiation, there was no break, no purge of any kind, and the corpora of state functionaries stayed in place. What also continued were inertias that date further back than Francoism. That's certainly the case for the judiciary, employment in which for some sagas has been practically a family tradition. The same is true for the diplomatic corps.

Can the same be said for the army?

No, it can't, thanks in large part to Spain's entry into NATO. At that point, the Spanish army became part of a global army. By now, the military is among the state bodies with the most academic degrees, the best language skills, and so forth.

But the judiciary is different.

Yes—because other factors have been in play as well. Opus Dei, for instance, has long managed to push its biggest talents into the judicial branch. The Spanish political Left has never done anything like that. Elsewhere in Europe, starting in the 1970s the Left began to suggest to some of its academic cadres that they consider a judicial career. Here in Spain, Opus Dei has had the field pretty much to itself.

You could see that as a failure on the part of the Socialist Party.

Curiously, the Socialist Party has never embraced Leninist principles when it comes to the importance of occupying the state. To be sure, the PSOE has managed to tie particular segments of the state apparatus to itself, especially the middle sectors, as well as of course the bulk of university professors. But the higher levels have always been more the territory of the Right. The same is true of the judicial branch.

Whose profile, therefore, is more conservative than that of the rest of Spanish society.

That's true for the upper echelons. At the level of the base, there has been a high level of rejuvenation, creating more diversity.

Would you say that the legitimacy of the courts has suffered as a result of the right-wing profile of those upper echelons? I suspect, for example, that in a place like Catalonia the Spanish judiciary doesn't have a particularly positive image.

In the case of Catalonia, there are other factors at play. Curiously, the Catalan middle classes, from the 1970s on, did not nudge their children toward careers in the central administration. Catalonia at that point was a very industrial society, in which the sons and daughters of the ruling classes were drawn to factories, businesses, or, if they studied law, a Barcelona law firm. Moving to Madrid to take up an administrative position was always a minority route. And by the 1980s, the administration of the autonomous region, the Generalitat, was providing jobs for people interested in a career as a state functionary.

Does Madrid feel that far away?

Not any farther than Paris feels to someone from Bordeaux, I'm sure. But what has happened is that the system of autonomous regions has made the central administration less diverse. By creating local administrative careers, it has reduced the presence in the central administration of individuals from elsewhere in the country. Which in turn has made it easier for that administration to continue in the same hands.

Speaking of diversity, what is it like to write about Spanish politics as a Catalan journalist? Is there something like a peripheral perspective that allows analysts from Catalonia, Valencia, the Basque Country, or Galicia to see things in Madrid differently?

Yes, there is something to that. I'll give you a recent example. My paper, *La Vanguardia*, has seen a sharp increase in online readership these past couple of months, when everyone has been confined to their houses. What I hear often is that people like reading us because we explain thing differently from the Madrid press. I think that's a crucial point. In a country as complex as Spain it's important to have a diversity of perspectives. One of the contributions we can make from Catalonia is to narrate Spain in a different way and make room for a real public discussion about how to understand this country. One of the great advantages of online journalism is that it provides much easier access to those different perspectives.

What exactly makes the Catalan perspective different?

First of all, we're not mixed up in the constant bar fight that is politics in Madrid. Or if we're mixed up in it, we are so differently. We're part of the system but not in the same way.

On the other hand, I've noticed that the lucidity that Catalans, Basques, or other observers from outside might display in Madrid disappears as soon as they have to deal with their own region.

The thing about local political systems is that they are very intense and very dense. Personally, they make me claustrophobic. I'm not kidding. If I'd have to return to Barcelona to write about Catalan politics, I'd have a very hard time of it. I don't think I could bear it psychologically. It's just too dense. What I like most is connecting things, relate them to the big picture. Even Spanish politics becomes boring after a while. At moments like these, in which we are facing a truly fundamental crisis, it's all the more important to know what's going on elsewhere: in Italy, in Germany, or in China for that matter. To understand what might happen in Spain in the next couple of years, for example, it is very important to understand the current state of mind of the German middle classes. A whole lot will depend on it.

Madrid, on the other hand, is mostly interested in itself.

It's one of the things that irritates me most about the Madrid media. Sometimes the city seems like a magnetic body that's so strong that no one is able to lift their feet off the ground. It's all Madrid all the time: "Did you hear what happened yesterday at the National Criminal Court?" Sure, what happened at the court might be important, but damn, what about the debate in Germany? Because that's what our future depends on!

The increased presence of peripheral voices and points of view in Madrid is a good thing, then, for Spain. You see it as something healthy.

Yes, I do. It helps to bring more variety and rigor. And it wasn't always like this. If you go back in the archive and look at *La Vanguardia* from the years of the Transition, you'll see that the coverage was almost entirely done by young journalists from Madrid, who'd set up their own agency to supply what they called the "regional press." Our paper, which had been part of the machinery of Francoism, had always had a good international coverage. But it was going through a process of *perestroika* and simply didn't have the manpower to cover events in Madrid.

The idea that an increased peripheral presence is healthy for Spain is not shared by a good part of the Spanish Right, which tends to construe peripheral voices and demands, especially from Catalonia and the Basque Country, as toxic to the body politic.

They see the peripheries as a disruption. On top of that, in the peripheries the Spanish Right loses its ability to operate as a dominant power.

Speaking of power and peripheries, what is going to happen in Catalonia in the next couple of years?

It's going to be complicated. The independence movement continues to be very convinced and emotionally very motivated, but the possibility for them to implement their program is nil at this point. They've maxed out on their electoral support and the years of European reconstruction ahead will leave no margin at all for territorial fractures of any kind. The independence movement, in other words, has some rewinding to do. But that's complicated. It's as if they got on a Ferris wheel that stopped suddenly due to an electrical failure—with them stuck at the very top. How do they get down? Who'll send for the fire truck and ladder?

And what if the fire truck has to come from Madrid?

Well, if Madrid was smart, it'd send that truck and ladder, and not beat the Catalans up once they've made it down. That's what would happen in a country less obsessed with revenge than Spain is. I doubt that will be possible given the current political climate. But we'll see. I don't rule anything out.

II

Antonio Maestre

*"The Transition Did Not Question the
Corporate Oligarchy"*

"This is a book about people who profited from, connived
with, and were committed to the dictatorship," the journalist Antonio Maestre writes in *Franquismo, S.A.* (Francoism,
Incorporated). "It is about those who preferred to take
advantage of the leg-up granted to them by crime" (2019a,
prologue). His book makes three explosive points. First, it
shows that many of the largest corporations, banks, and
family fortunes in Spain today—including Catalonia and
the Basque Country—owe much of their current power and
wealth to the Franco dictatorship and, often, to their active
intervention on the Nationalists' behalf in the Spanish Civil
War. The beneficial treatment they received from the regime
included market manipulation, concessions of (near) monopolies, and the use of prison labor. Their financial hegemony, the book shows, was further strengthened through
strategic mergers and alliances, often through marriage.

Second, Maestre makes clear that these companies and families have done their best to conceal the Francoist genealogy of their wealth. Although they benefited handsomely from the state, ironically many have since pushed to reduce the role of the state in economic life in favor of entrepreneurship, self-reliance, privatization, and other articles of neoliberal faith.

In the third place, Maestre explains that the Spanish state, the judiciary, and the media have never held these families and companies accountable. Unlike what has happened in Germany and other countries, they have never had to explain the immoral and illegitimate origins of their wealth and power. As a result, in Spain there has never been an acknowledgment of complicity, let alone attempts to issue apologies or reparations to the victims. *Franquismo, S.A.* came out in November 2019, right around the time of Franco's exhumation, and became an instant bestseller. In early February 2020, I sat down with Maestre for an interview.

If your book has a plotline, it is one that emphasizes continuities: you show that those who came to occupy the heights of economic power during the Franco regime were able to maintain that position through the democratic transition. Yet if they managed to survive, in a Darwinian sense, it must also have been because they were able to adapt to the country's new political reality. How did they pull that off?

The truth of the matter is that it was not difficult for them at all, because hardly anything changed. The truth is that their power and capital were never questioned. No one asked them about the origins of their wealth. All they had to do after the transition was to move close to whomever was in power. In the book, I show how José María de Oriol Urquijo went about this. Urquijo had been one of the central backers of the fascist revolt of 1936. During Franco's rule, he was handsomely rewarded for that support with a series of high-level positions. In 1941, he assumed the leadership of Iberdrola, which later became the country's largest electrical company, and in 1955 he was appointed *procurador de las Cortes* [a member of Franco's non-elected parliament]. After the Socialists came to power in 1982, he simply cozied up to Felipe González, the Socialist Prime Minister, in order to continue to conduct his business with Iberdrola.

What his case illustrates is that the democratic transition never once questioned the corporate oligarchy that flourished under Francoism. The financial power structures were simply left intact. The corporate elite did not even have to change the way it interacted with the political class. Since the systemic corruption of the Franco regime also remained in place, companies could stick to their same old modus operandi. Another good example is that of Juan-Miguel Villar Mir, who still today heads up one of the country's largest construction companies. He was one of the top corporate oligarchs during the dictatorship. In recent years, Villar Mir has been indicted for his company's involvement in a massive bribe scheme set up to finance the Partido Popular. In exchange for government contracts, Villar Mir would kick back one percent of the contracts' value to the party coffers.

I understand that the political class, out of passivity or self-interest, helped perpetuate Francoist economic elites without any form of accountability or reparation. But haven't the media been equally complicit?

Yes, of course. And in fact, the royal family, too, has been a key piece of the puzzle. When it comes to maintaining the economic power of the Francoist elites, the monarchy has played a central role. The country's wealthiest families practically belonged to the court, and major business transactions were conducted with the connivance of the King. But for many years, the mainstream media upheld a tacit agreement never to question the monarchy. To make things worse, the press has also been under the direct control of the economic elites, who tend to hold major stakes in media companies. Media power and economic power, in other words, have been closely intertwined, with little to no room for independent movement. To be sure, the crisis of 2008 has created some openings for media outlets with different political cultures. But from the Transition until then, all the important media were tied to the economic elites. Even a newspaper like *El País*, over time, has maintained the status quo, showing a clear preference for defending privilege rather than questioning it. Which is perhaps not surprising, given that the founders and leadership of *El País* came from a Falangist background.

How about the judiciary?

The judiciary is one of the most glaring cases of Francoist continuity. While in politics the return of free elections implied new actors joining the stage, in the courts there wasn't even a change of cast. The very same judges who were in place under Francoism continued working after the transition. The same is true for some judicial institutions, such as Franco's Court of Public Order, which simply changed its name to become the Audiencia Nacional. The judiciary, like the military and the police, didn't have to do much more than adapt to the new way of doing things. In some cases that took longer than in others. During the transition, the police and the courts were as repressive and antidemocratic as they'd been during the dictatorship. And that lasted for a while.

The economic elites' holding on to power can be explained as a function of their material or economic interest. Was the complicity of the courts and the police more ideological in nature, given that judges and police officers had been formed by, and sworn loyalty to, the Francoist state?

Yes, completely. The economic elites simply wanted to continue to make money, and they were able to do so because the Transition never threatened their privileges. The courts and the police came from serving in a repressive regime. Not only were they ideologically in tune with that regime, but they'd also learned to operate based on repression. The same judge that in 1974 tried Communists as enemies of the state continued to occupy the bench years later, without any form of purge or reeducation. Meanwhile, the abuses and murders committed by the police in the years of the Transition went largely unpunished.

Let's pivot to the future. In your book you compare Spain to Germany, which had investigations and reparations, although it took

*the country a long time to get there. In Spain, nothing of the kind
has happened yet. Yet recently the new government has said it would
like to initiate a process to return property and funds that were expropriated during and after the war from those who had remained
loyal to the Republican government. I wonder what the first steps
of such a process would look like. You have recently argued, for
example, that it doesn't make sense to make extolling Francoism
punishable by law, as Spain's current government also proposes to
do, if there is no jurisprudence yet to establish the illegitimacy of the
Franco regime to begin with. What's the proper order of operations
to begin working toward some form of economic transitional justice?*

First, there are laws that need to be revoked, laws that were
instituted by Francoism and that the transition simply left
untouched. Next, the effects of those laws on the citizenry
need to be reversed. Take for example the Ley de Incau-
tación de Bienes Materiales (Law to Seize Material Goods),
from 1937. By this law, if you were Republican and the
courts decided you had committed high treason—that is,
you had not supported the Francoist coup—then all your
possessions were seized by the state. What clearly needs to
happen first is to annul that law and undo its consequences—
that is, to return what was expropriated to its rightful owners. Of course, this is very complicated, because the goods
and properties that were seized may have been bought and
sold since then.

Another key measure is to extend the judicial status of
victim to the victims of the Franco regime and its repressive
sentences. Currently, only those killed by terrorism after
1968—that is, after ETA began its attacks on the Francoist
state—have that status. Those who were killed or persecuted

by the regime may have the symbolic status of victims, but they lack judicial standing as such. That also means they can make no claims for reparation, let alone demand that their seized assets be returned.

Third, it is key that the 1977 amnesty law be revoked. All three of these measures would help establish the juridical framework to begin investigating the Francoist expropriations. Once that framework is in place, however, it may well be possible to simply follow existing legislation—the current criminal code—to pursue reparations and returns. We'll have to see.

This is the process that Germany followed. The Germans did not start by criminalizing the apology or denial of genocide. No, they first followed a juridical process to create the conditions in which such a law would have effect, which is what the trials at Nuremberg and Auschwitz helped do. You can't say that extolling Francoism is a crime if the regime's criminal nature has not been established by the courts. In West Germany, it was decided that any law from the Nazi period that conflicted with the federal constitution would be annulled de facto. In Spain, by contrast, Francoist legislation was left in place, like the infamous Law of Official Secrets, which dates from 1968.

The way you put it, it sounds like establishing this juridical framework would make reparations or returns relatively simple.

Sure, it would make cultural, moral, and economic reparations much more straightforward. But don't forget that changing the framework along these lines would end up calling into question the entire current structure of the state as we know it—that is, as it was established during the Transition. On its own, just revoking the Amnesty law would be nothing short of a judicial revolution—among other things, it would mean that many former officials who are still alive could be indicted. More importantly, revoking the Francoist laws that justified expropriations of capital and goods would imply that a lot of the country's wealth would have to change hands. I strongly doubt that the government is ready to do this. I think its goal is a form of reparation that is more symbolic or aesthetic rather than really addressing the structural issues.

Your book provides a detailed genealogy of economic power. That seems to imply a political position: namely, the idea that in order to understand and address current forms of injustice, it is necessary to turn to the past for explanations. An alternative position would be to say that the tendency of economic elites to perpetuate their power—a power accrued and maintained through the complicity of the political and media elites—is not limited to Spain. It is par for the course around the globe. Is it really necessary to explain the current state of affairs as a legacy of Francoism? Doesn't that allow the Right to dismiss you as someone obsessed with the past and bent on winning a war that was lost eighty years ago?

The central problem for the Spanish case is the total lack of knowledge about this genealogy. In other countries there has been some form investigation and reparation and, more importantly, some form of moral condemnation. This kind of condemnation, I think, is important to build a stronger democracy, a democracy based on the guarantee of non-repetition. For this to occur in Spain, it is necessary to have a debate about the ways that wealth was accumulated during the war and the dictatorship. You are right to point out that those processes were, in the end, not all that different from those that have occurred elsewhere in the capitalist world. Nevertheless, if you look at Germany, you see how powerful it can be for those involved when there is a form of social censure of certain practices, along with reparations for harm inflicted and even an occasional court conviction. By establishing the truth about the way wealth was accumulated, what such a process does is to build a society in which certain practices are marked as subject to moral condemnation. In Spain, this hasn't happened. My book tries to kick off this debate and begin building the collective awareness that would allow for a moral sanction of this kind. Look, I'm realistic enough to know that a full financial reparation is impossible. But what we can do is to make this a subject of public debate, to establish the truth and make sure that truth carries weight as we build a healthier democracy.

Your book also provides a powerful counterargument against those on the Right who wield self-reliance and the free market as arguments to reduce the power and size of the state.

It is very important to make clear that many of those who today appeal to meritocracy and economic liberalism in order to reduce the public sector owe their own massive wealth to a very strong—and very repressive—state that, for almost forty years, privileged a handful of elites who enriched themselves to perverse extents without having to compete in a free market, just because they had helped support a military coup against a legitimately elected government.

1 2

The Media

"This is not a time for neutrality," the minister of the interior told the editor of *El Mundo*, Spain's third-largest newspaper, in the fall of 2015. "The country is facing powerful enemies," he said. "Can we count on you?" David Jiménez, who'd come back to Spain to assume the editorship of *El Mundo* after many years reporting from abroad, couldn't believe his ears (2019, chapter 4). Yet everyone else seemed to accept the government's brazen attempt at cooptation as par for the course. Jiménez, indignant, at first rebuffed the Minister. But then his paper was blacklisted and stopped receiving leaks from the ministry and the national police. Sometime later, when Jiménez visited again, this time in the company of his publisher, the minister gave them a second chance. He passed them a valuable leak—a tip about Catalan politicians receiving illegal commissions—but immediately had two asks in return: he wanted the paper to run a news item about police medals, and he requested that the journalist covering the ministry for *El Mundo* be reassigned. Jiménez, once more, was taken aback. "I was getting tired of the obsession politicians had with organizing my team for me," he writes in his memoir, *El director* (The editor), which came out in 2019 (chapter 6).

The book is a disenchanted exposé of everything that's wrong with mainstream journalism in Spain today. Among other things, Jiménez reveals that major media outlets have longstanding agreements with large banks and corporations based on a simple quid pro quo: in exchange for generous monetary support—nominally for advertisement—companies buy the right to preferential treatment from the media in the form of friendly coverage, a direct line to the newsroom, and journalistic self-censorship. "The exchange of favors between the press and corporations had been established for so long that it wasn't even necessary for the board rooms to pick up the phone to reinforce their part of the deal," Jiménez writes; "the newsrooms had internalized the fact that companies like Telefónica, the Banco Santander, or El Corte Inglés were untouchable" (chapter 7).

Soon after his return, Jiménez started receiving invitations to join *tertulias*, the live group debates on Spanish radio and television that make up the bulk of daily political coverage and tend to draw large audiences. The format is the same across networks: an anchor nominally moderates heated exchanges among up to eight leading journalists and media personalities about the controversies of the day. "Your seat is part of the open quota," Jiménez was told before one of his first appearances. When he asked what that meant, he was told that he was one of the few participants who'd been picked by the network. As it turned out, the bulk of the line-ups for these debates are negotiated in advance with political parties—even with intra-party factions.

Each gets to place their own people, who are expected to defend their sponsors' talking points, which are sometimes fed to them while they are on air. Few viewers and listeners are aware of these manipulations.

In addition to revealing shenanigans like these, Jiménez's memoir also gives a peek into what has become known as *las cloacas*, the sewers, a longstanding secret network of operators from the police, the media, and the government that fabricates fake news in order to discredit political rivals. A central figure in the plot is José Manuel Villarejo, a police chief—now retired and indicted—who started his career during the tail end of Francoism as a police officer stationed in the Basque Country. As he worked his way up the ladder, he began taking jobs under the radar for political and business leaders. At the same time, he collected a vast archive of compromising materials, particularly audio recordings, on everybody he interacted with. A mix between Dirty Harry and J. Edgar Hoover, Villarejo used his extensive network to accumulate unprecedented power and, over time, considerable wealth. As the go-to confidant, operator, and all-round intelligence handyman for executives and politicians on the Left and Right, he became all but untouchable. (He's spent time in prison since 2017, but even there, Gorka Castillo reported in February 2020, he was treated like a king.)

The media's dependency on figures like Villarejo, Jiménez writes, means that news scoops presented as investigative journalism are rarely more than carefully orchestrated leaks with little to no follow-up or fact-checking; the leaker even gets to decide when and how the story will run. In 2015 and 2016, as the emergence of new political parties like Podemos and the ballooning Catalan independence movement were seen to threaten the status quo, *las cloacas* went into overdrive, culminating, among other things, in a widely published police report that claimed Podemos had been financed by Venezuela and that its leader, Pablo Iglesias, had large sums stashed away in a tax haven. By the time the whole thing was proven to be an invention from *las cloacas*, the electoral damage had been done (Jiménez 2019, chapter 6).

Other highlights from Villarejo's shadowy career include a fictitious report on Judge Baltasar Garzón from the early 1990s—when Garzón was investigating the use of secret government funds to finance a dirty war against ETA, which was waging a terrorist campaign for Basque independence—in which the judge was associated with drug traffickers and orgies. "All of it seems lifted straight from the plot of a B-movie," Garzón, whose interaction with Villarejo became more friendly in later years, said in a recent interview (Roures i Lop 2017, 33:10).

In light of these revelations, it is no surprise that Spaniards distrust their journalists almost as much as their politicians. In its 2015 *Digital News Report*, Reuters reported that Spaniards trusted their media less than any of the other European countries polled (Reuters 2015). By 2019, Spain's relative ranking had improved, albeit partly due to the fact that trust in the media elsewhere had plummeted.[1] "The media in Spain are extremely polarized," Magda Bandera, editor of the magazine *La Marea*, told me in early 2020. "I am certain that the levels of manipulation here exceed those

---

1. What follows relies on reporting done with Bécquer Seguín, which has appeared in *The Nation* (Faber and Seguín 2015) and the contributed volume *Spain after the Indignados/15M Movement*, edited by Steven Torres and Óscar Pereira-Zazo (Faber and Seguín 2019).

in neighboring democracies. People take for granted that journalism is a form of political trench warfare."

Although Spain boasts more than eighty newspapers and a broad range of television and radio channels, the bulk of these media is controlled by large, transnational corporate conglomerates. The PRISA group includes the newspaper *El País* alongside a slew of magazines and TV and radio networks and production companies (and until 2014 a trans-Atlantic publishing giant). The second largest group, Vocento, controls the national, right-wing (royalist and Catholic) newspaper *ABC* plus an additional thirteen smaller papers. Planeta is the largest Spanish-language publishing company in the world, but it also deals in television and controls *La Razón*, a relatively small newspaper that owes its high profile to its position on the far right of the political spectrum. While many of the conglomerates started out as family businesses—often families that benefited from close ties with the Franco regime—they are now controlled by transnational corporations or a handful of powerful financial institutions (Serrano 2010, 141).

Over the past twenty years, dwindling advertising revenue has put these corporations under heavy pressure. The Great Recession led to spiking debts. Massive layoffs satisfied shareholders' desire for short-term profits. Meanwhile, the astronomical compensation packages for CEOs went untouched. When Bécquer Seguín and I reported on the state of the Spanish media for *The Nation* in 2015, we found that the conglomerates' debt problem had directly curbed reporters' freedom. "Since the 2008 crisis, the banks have converted the media's debt into company shares," former *El País* reporter Guillem Martínez explained. "They have become the owners and exercise their role in nineteenth-century style." Martínez remembered an instance in 2013 when a banking executive called up an editor and told him to fire a journalist who was tweeting critically about the bank. "I have worked for outlets where I've been told not to mention anything bad about a certain company or about such and such politician," Mar Cabra, who has worked for the International Consortium of Investigative Journalists (ICIJ), told us. "It was seen as normal. Some companies or some political parties were just taboo because of the outlet's affinity with them or because they were a big advertiser." Anecdotes like these fully confirm the practices that Jiménez reveals in his memoir.

If on one side the media are controlled by corporations, on the other they are under pressure from regional and national authorities, who have long used their advertising budgets and subsidy schemes to control television, radio, and print media. Political parties in power subsidize privately owned media directly or indirectly in exchange for political support. "The political clientelism of some of the private media," José Sanclemente wrote in *ElDiario.es*, a relatively new media outlet, "is proportional to the amount of financial support injected into them from the public coffers" (2015). "There are clear grounds to suspect that the national and regional governments play favorites when it comes to advertising contracts, licensing, and subsidies," added David Cabo from Civio, a nonprofit pushing for transparency and open access to public data, in an interview. Journalist Trinidad Deiros agreed. "In Spain, journalism has traditionally been a very polarized profession, under the thumb of the powers that be," she told us. "The most extreme manifestation of this deplorable situation is the shameful political manipulation of the state-run media. Agencies like EFE or TVE, which should be a neutral public service, have almost always been turned into mouthpieces of the governing party." In the end, Deiros said, "the Spanish media bear a great similarity to the system in which they have flourished since the death of dictator Franco: a democracy with a whiff of authoritarianism, in which citizen participation has been reduced to a bare minimum."

The media's vulnerabilities are many, David Jiménez explains in his memoir. As elsewhere in the world, their financial challenges have mounted, especially since the digital revolution and the Great Recession. In a landscape dominated by plunging print runs and seemingly endless layoffs, reporters and editors have naturally become more risk-averse. But in Spain, two additional factors are in play. First, the unusually high level of codependency—if not outright promiscuity—among the media, the corporate world, and the political leadership; and second, the relative weakness of professional ethics among the country's journalists. Both reflect the long shadow of Francoism, Trinidad Deiros told us: "Ours is a political culture obsessed with controlling information. This is a legacy of a very opaque transition to democracy that did not break with the dictatorship and therefore inherited some of its vices. Almost all of us— journalists, politicians, militants from left and right, citizens in general—have grown up in this context. And it has only begun to change very recently. It'll take years before we lose that terrible fear of free and truthful information."

The tight economic and political control handicapping the written media is even more present in the audiovisual arena. Spain's state-owned television channels, Televisión Española, operate at the nationwide level, while regional autonomous communities, such as Catalonia, Galicia, and Basque Country, have channels that broadcast in their respective languages. Additionally, there exist commercial, conglomerate-owned channels, which command about 80 percent of the market. It is widely known that the governments exploit the television channels they control to their own benefit, resulting in highly skewed news reporting.

Guillem Martínez sees a deeper-seated cultural problem. "The Regime of 1978 cannot cohabitate with independent media. In other cultures, big scandals like the ones Spain has seen would have meant the end of the monarchy, the PP, the PSOE, or Convergència, from Catalonia. They would have sparked a political earthquake that has not happened here, nor in the media," he said. "The media, in other words, forms an important part of the regime, or the system, or whatever you want to call it. And whether it is due to culture, or to local dynamics, I don't always see the Left really wishing for a different type of culture or a different type of media. Rather, they would like their own direct, vertical access to them, just like everyone else." Martínez wants to see the Spanish media embrace a much more critical approach to those in power: "I strongly believe that Spain needs one or several media, print media, that swim against the tide of the local culture." Yet he doesn't believe projects like that have a high chance of survival.

Still, the Great Recession and its massive layoffs fueled the birth of a host of new media outlets with exactly this ambition. In part because they include groups of veteran journalists, they are anything but naïve. In fact, they have themselves taken on a leading role in denouncing less-than-savory journalistic practices and exposing the network of political and economic interests that curb journalistic freedom in Spain. Of the new independent media outlets that have emerged in recent years, *ElDiario.es* is no doubt the most successful. It is the brainchild of Ignacio Escolar, who in 2007 was the founding director of *Público*, a print daily that quickly managed to carve out a space to the left of *El País*. *Público* distinguished itself from the latter by daring to break longstanding taboos, including the ban on critical coverage of the monarchy. The paper also voiced strong opposition to the 2011 constitutional amendment that privileged paying down the national debt over social spending. But *Público* was funded by a corporate owner, the Catalan media magnate Jaume Roures, who in January 2012 decided to shut down its print edition, leaving most of the reporting and editorial staff jobless. (*Público* continues to exist today as an online news site.) Many of the laid-off reporters and editors turned their disillusion and frustration into action and went on to organize startup venues with a renewed commitment to high journalistic standards and, especially, to total and rigorous independence from political and commercial interests.

These new venues operate according to several different models. The online daily *InfoLibre*, for example, focuses on investigative reporting—often publishing fewer than half a dozen new stories per day—and opinion. Run by former *Público* editors Manuel Rico and Jesús Maraña, *InfoLibre* has associated itself with *Mediapart*, a French online outlet for investigative journalism, and, like its French partner, it subsists on subscription fees. "We defend the idea that information has a value," Rico told us in 2015. "And that means one of two things: the readers pay, or the large corporations do." The second option is off the table, Rico said. "We strictly reject hidden advertising agreements with large corporations." *ElDiario.es*, by contrast, is more ambitious and sprawling, with a tightly organized newsroom, a broad stable of bloggers, and several regional branches. Its business model relies on both advertising and a membership subscription scheme that is not quite a paywall. *Contexto* is an online weekly without a paywall that combines long-form reporting with interviews and opinion pieces. The goal of its fourteen founding editors—many of them experienced journalists fed up with the mainstream media— was to return to the fundamentals of independent journalism. "We don't do breaking news, nor do we run rehashed pieces from the agencies," its editor, Miguel Mora, told us. "We don't compete to be the first, and we don't mix texts with videos and entertainment. Our focus is minimalist. We intend to respect the basic tenets of classical journalism: we only publish our own stories, written where the news happens." Representing yet another model is *La Marea*, a smaller outfit that combines a freely accessible daily online site with a bimonthly paper edition. Initially set up as a reporter-owned, assembly-based cooperative with over one hundred co-owners, *La Marea*'s editors took the principled—and expensive—decision never to accept politically objectionable advertising. The paper subsists primarily on readers' subscription fees. It works with a minimal salaried staff and relies primarily on freelance contributors.

The emergence of the new independent media in Spain is closely linked with the critical view of Spain's Transition

that historians, journalists, and political parties such as Podemos have ushered into mainstream discourse. Business
models aside, what *InfoLibre*, *La Marea*, and *ElDiario.es* share
is the conviction that the political and economic structures
produced by the Transition have not allowed for the config-
uration of a media landscape conducive to a healthy democratic culture in which those in power are held accountable
on an ongoing basis. And unlike the political mainstream
of Spain's transition culture, they explicitly declare themselves republican, feminist, and antifascist.

FURTHER READING

The most comprehensive critical analyses of the evolution of
the Spanish media landscape have been written by Serrano
(2010, 2012). For a well-written history of Spain's newspaper
of record, *El País*, and the media conglomerate it birthed,
see Cruz Seoane and Sueiro (2004). In addition to Jiménez,
other leading Spanish journalists and editors have also written revealing memoirs; among them is Cebrián (2016).

13
Cristina Fallarás

"Francoism Never Went Away"

In 2012, Cristina Fallarás, one of Spain's leading feminists and most successful news editors, was evicted from her home because she could no longer afford the mortgage. Four years earlier, she'd been laid off from her post as associate editor of the newspaper *ADN*, in one of the first of many mass firings that would hit the Spanish media sector in the wake of the Great Recession. Throughout this period, Fallarás continued to appear in television and radio debates, as both a victim and an analyst of the Spanish crisis. Her memoir about these years, *A la puta calle: Crónica de un desahucio* (Out on the fucking street: Chronicle of an eviction), came out in 2013.

Born in 1968 in Zaragoza, Fallarás studied journalism in Barcelona. She served as editor of *El Mundo*'s Catalan edition and the digital daily *Diario 16*. As an activist, she's been a prominent voice for a range of progressive causes, from the rights of the victims of Francoism to media reform and

making prostitution illegal. In 2018, in the wake of a controversial court decision involving a gang rape, she coined the
hashtag #Cuéntalo, which launched the Spanish-language
version of the #MeToo movement, as hundreds of thousands of women came out about their experiences with
sexual assault. Fallarás has also authored six novels. I spoke
with her in February 2020.

———————

*Those who have written critically about the Spanish media have
pointed to journalists' improperly close relationship with political
and corporate power holders. Politicians and CEOs, it seems, regularly help shape what gets covered and how. Do you see this as a
holdover from Francoism, or rather as a distinguishing feature of
post-Franco democracy?*

The first thing to remember is that Spain's large corporations were built on Francoist state repression: executions,
imprisonment, expropriations, and Republican slave labor.
That said, the media's attitude today toward Francoism and
its continued presence has been much more worrisome.
It can be summarized in one word: silence. For the past
forty years, the media have *not* covered what's going on at
the Valley of the Fallen; not covered the fact that this is a
country littered with mass graves with tens of thousands
of victims; or the fact that Franco and his family enriched
themselves immensely during the war and the dictatorship.
To be sure, the media have covered political corruption;
but again, it's interesting to see that those who ended up
tried and convicted have been the politicians but not the
entities that bribed them in exchange for massive public

contracts—namely, the large corporations, especially those that were established during the dictatorship. In this way, political corruption has served to feed the continuation of Francoism in Spain.

But hasn't the media coverage changed a lot in recent years? Hasn't that silence by now been broken?

Sure, in the last couple of years the media have begun mentioning the fact that the Spanish state was spending tax money to maintain Franco's tomb and put fresh flowers on it every day. It's also true that, by now, the media discuss the need to exhume the mass graves; or the story of the thousands of Spanish Republicans who were deported to Nazi camps. Or the massive fortune of the Franco family, amassed by stealing land, money, and real estate, and the fact that some of the individuals who tortured for the regime continue to enjoy their decorations and generous state pensions. But this change in patterns of media coverage has only happened recently. And the media have changed quite reluctantly, largely because of the tremendous pressure applied through social media by a heavily organized civil society.

In other words, you do not see a real change in attitude in the media sector.

No, not at all. Much like we've seen with #MeToo, it was grassroots demands that forced the media to finally pick up the story. Why are they now covering violence against women more prominently? Because of our overwhelming social-media campaigns. The same goes for the legacies of Francoism.

Look, I always say that the editor is not the one who calls the shots. The editor is the one who obeys most readily. The real problem in the Spanish media are not the journalists; it's the corporate boards. Take *El País*, which is often thought of as one of the more progressive papers, much like the radio network *Cadena Ser*, owned by the same PRISA conglomerate. PRISA's board is packed not only with holdovers from Francoism, but also with representatives of large corporations that come from Francoist money and the Catholic hierarchy.

A hierarchy that still wields significant power, despite the nominal separation between church and state.

The central role that the Church, its lobby, and its clergy continue to play in Spain is unparalleled anywhere else. It's even worse than Poland, Ireland, or Latin America. The presence of the Church in the media sector is immense. And don't forget: the Catholic Church was *the* pillar buttressing Franco's regime. So much so, that it makes more sense to think of Francoism as a Catholic dictatorship rather than a military regime.

All of which, I imagine, only complicates the everyday life of the Spanish journalist. To guard themselves against these threats, it seems to me, journalists would have to rely on two things: a relative financial independence and a commitment to professional ethics. Neither seem particularly strong in Spain.

There has been very little of both, although the situation has been improving somewhat after 2011, with the appearance of new independent digital outlets and the emergence of new political parties like Podemos. It's become harder for the media to be silent about the big issues they left under-covered for years.

A third line of defense for journalists under pressure would be the judiciary, in its role as a guarantor of press freedom and the population's constitutional right to truthful information. What role have the courts played, in your view?

The problem is that the judiciary, too, comes straight from Francoism. Just look at the courts' refusal to try Francoist torturers for crimes against humanity, despite international law stipulating that those types of crimes have no statute of limitations and cannot be subject to amnesties of any kind. How do you explain that the Spanish courts were able to go after Pinochet, the former dictator of Chile, but cannot try the crimes of Francoism? Or that the Spanish state has not paid a dime to exhume the hundreds of thousands of victims from the Civil War who are still in mass graves?

Antonio Maestre has pointed out that the establishment has a lot to lose. Rescinding the amnesty law would also clear the way for damage claims.

That, indeed, is the big problem. There is a huge fear. What Franco instituted, after all, was a regime of larceny. Those in power applied themselves thoroughly to stealing whatever they could: land, buildings, companies, homes, property, huge estates. That loot has ended up in the hands of what are still today the country's most powerful corporations and families. It's no coincidence that, in the wake of Franco's exhumation, calls have been increasing to investigate the family's assets and return stolen property to its rightful owners. In Germany, companies that profited from slave labor under the Nazi regime were forced to pay reparations. Here, the regime lasted much longer. Imagine the number of people that were employed under slave-like conditions, in all sectors of the economy, not just infrastructure and construction, but also in the cultural industry, including the Grupo Planeta, the country's largest publisher. Reparations to the victims and their families would be astronomical.

What do you mean, forced labor at Planeta?

For years, there were writers, editors, proofreaders, and translators who worked for free, or practically free, to avoid retaliations or being denounced. Manuel Vázquez Montalbán always said that he began his career working for free, based on a deal: "If you work, I'll keep my mouth shut."

The way you describe it, the only road to improvement, be it in the media or in politics, is through grassroots pressure. What role do you see here for the feminist movement, also in relation to the legacies of Francoism?

That pressure is significant. It's important to understand that Spanish feminism today is a very well-organized movement with broad networks of thousands upon thousands of women. We are not just intervening in the debate about gender violence, which is huge, but also in other debates, including those related to Francoism, whether it's reparations, the role of the courts, or the media silence. We constantly call out complicities. After all, the judiciary and the media have not merely been silent, they've been in connivance with the Francoist economic elites.

Ignacio Echevarría has written that the Left has tended to exaggerate, or misperceive, the Francoist roots of the Right. Parties like Vox and the PP, he says, have more in common with their European counterparts than that they are indebted to Francoism.

I'm sorry, but I completely disagree. Vox, in my view, is an exception in the landscape of the European Far Right. For one, because it's an ultra-Catholic party, funded by the Church. Unlike what we see in France or Germany, its voters are much less concerned with immigration than with recovering the values of the Catholic Church and with stopping feminism in its tracks. This reflects the Church's attempt to recover its control over women's bodies, in the same way that it's fighting to continue its control over public education. You have to remember: Francoism, in Spain, has never been tried in court. It never went away. Its flame has been kept burning by the Church, the large corporations which came from the regime, and the Spanish Right. Vox emerges from that triad.

14
Marije Hristova

*"Many in the Movement Still See
Memory as Equivalent to Truth"*

Marije Hristova has spent more than fifteen years studying the way Spain remembers the Civil War and the Franco dictatorship. Her doctoral dissertation (2016) considered the way transnational memories shaped the emerging memory movement in Spain; since then, she's been a member of the research group Unsettling Remembering and Social Cohesion in Transnational Europe (UNREST) at the Spanish National Research Council, and a research fellow in the project "The Underground Past," led by Francisco Ferrándiz. She is also a founding member of the Spanish association *Memorias en Red*, which organizes debates, exhibitions, and events related to the topic of remembrance. Born and raised in the Netherlands, she's lived in Spain for close to ten years. I interviewed her in early 2020.

You've experienced the evolution of Spain's memory movement from up close. Since its emergence around the year 2000, much has changed, thanks in large part to its tireless activism. And yet, the initial sense that Spain has a whole lot of unfinished business seems to have remained.

There has been a lot of activism, it's true, but Spain has never had a proper debate about what a politics of memory might look like. While many activists in the movement have focused on the judicial route, few have demanded a politics of memory. Sure, they have protested many things and succeeded in having remnants of Francoism removed from public spaces. But there has been little movement beyond that. As a result, many of them continue to have the impression that things are stagnant, although, like you say, a whole lot has changed if you compare the situation today with twenty years ago.

What, then, explains this impression of stagnation?

Many in the movement still see memory as equivalent to truth. The goal is to finally tell the story of what *really* happened during the Civil War and the dictatorship and to get that story out there, into the public sphere and the history textbooks, so that everything that's always been kept hidden or silenced will finally become public. This conception of memory has made it difficult to have a real discussion about what distinguishes memory from history. It's made it hard to home in on the *public* dimension of memory, but also to acknowledge its inherent multiplicity. Historical, or better, collective memory, in the end, is a form of publicly narrating the past. But it's never a single narrative.

Given these complications, how do you feel about a hypothetical national museum of the Civil War and Francoism?

I am instinctively suspicious of all top-down forms of memory. The whole idea of collective memory is that many different narratives coexist. As soon as the state gets involved, that multiplicity is in danger. And yet in the Spanish case, I think that a museum of that sort would go a long way toward satisfying the demands of the memory movement. It'd be a very tangible form of recognition. The currently existing museums, which are almost all small and grassroots, can't fulfill that role. Nor, for that matter, could a museum in Catalonia or the Basque Country. It would have to be in Madrid.

While the memory movement seems to equate memory to truth, I have the impression that, for the political class, a national museum holds the promise of closure: the end to the decades' worth of memory battles. When Pedro Sánchez first announced Franco's exhumation, he said the Valley should become a space for "reconciliation"—an idea that goes right back to the Transition and the amnesty law.

If the Spanish state would develop a sound politics of memory, that could well lead to a form of reconciliation. But the PSOE, in my mind, is still stuck in the template that starts from the notion that both sides committed evil acts in the war and connects it to the idea that stating that position publicly will lead to reconciliation. "If everyone was to blame, then we can be reconciled." But I don't think a narrative like that leads to reconciliation. Putting everyone on the same level—we're all perpetrators and we're all victims—is too low a bar. I think reconciliation demands an acknowledgment of the other, and an acknowledgment of mistakes made. And in that sense, both sides are not on the same level at all. What do we mean when we talk about reconciliation? Thinking from the field of transitional justice, it means that a society can move on after a conflict and continue to live together.

From that perspective, would you say reconciliation has been achieved in Spain?

For part of the population, it has not.

What would a reconciled Spain look like?

That is a hard question. It may be that, in a reconciled Spain, the Civil War would no longer be instrumentalized politically. Today, anytime the war comes up, it immediately produces two positions that are irreconcilable. This blocks all possibility of progress or political consensus, even in areas like education, which should be a normal part of any democratic society.

Does the tendency to retrace Spain's current problems to Francoism or the Transition contribute to this stalemate?

While it's true that Francoism is still everywhere, I do think that constantly going back to those Civil War positions is an obstacle. In my experience, sociological Francoism is constantly present in Spain as a dividing element, even when not everyone encounters it every day. As soon as you scratch the surface, the division appears.

How much of that division is due to the central place that political affiliation plays in Spaniards' identity? I sometimes get the impression that voters identify with their party as if it were a football club. Another element I've seen operate is the equation of political identity with family loyalty. People feel they can't condemn Francoism if that means condemning their parents or grandparents.

I am not sure those are such crucial factors. Sure, family structures are important in a society like Spain, where so much depends on personal relations. But I know plenty of people whose families include both Left and Right genealogies. And there are many who do not identify with the politics of their family, especially among younger generations. Looking toward the future, I see change and progress. Even just in my academic field of history and memory, I think that things will change significantly when the generation who is now between thirty and forty years old gets to occupy academic chairs and professorships. These younger researchers have been able to think much further than the older generations of scholars. They've also established more connections with similar discussions going on elsewhere in the world. That allows them, in turn, to look at Spain differently.

What areas do you feel would benefit most by a more intentional form of memory politics originating from the state?

History education, for one. But also, the management of public space, including monuments. Despite all the activism there has been little activity in that regard. Sure, Francoist symbols have been removed. But so far little has been put in their place. If you focus almost exclusively on removal, you run the risk of ending up with a vacuum in which the past is not talked about at all. A third important area are museums, which after all are public spaces that tell a story about the past.

Can you think of museums elsewhere that may serve as an inspiration for Spain?

There is a memory museum in Chile, a modern building whose focus is very community-driven and that also serves as an archive. It resists imposing a single, finished narrative. Those two elements, permeability to the community and avoiding the suggestion of a single voice, a single truth, can serve as an example for Spain. On the other hand, I often wonder whether this multiplicity of voices, the absence of a single narrative, would work in the long run. Doesn't it take us too far from the truth that the activists are seeking? I find it hard, even as a researcher, to strike that balance. On the one hand, there are many stories, many points of view. On the other, there are the victims and their suffering, clamoring to be recognized. How do you position yourself ethically between those two poles, especially in times of fake news and post-truth?

Ricard Vinyes would say: The multiplicity of voices is fine, it's actually what you want—as long as you agree on the core values of democracy. All memories have a right to be narrated, but those core values allow us to not give all those narrations the same ethical status. There can be no moral equation between the memory of the struggle against democracy and the memory of the struggle for democracy.

This reminds me of the EU-wide project UNREST of which I was a part for several years, which organized itself around the concept of agonistic memory. Agonistic memory privileges representations of past conflict that are politicized, inviting the present to acknowledge the political passions that drove the people who were engaged in those conflicts. The project culminated in a museum exhibit. To be honest, I found it unconvincing. In the end, it was about little more than juxtaposing different points of view on war—including those of victims and perpetrators—that never jelled into a story of any kind. Memory, to work, must take the shape of a narration, and this wasn't it. On the other hand, I agree that a single story is not desirable, either. You can tell I still haven't figured it out.

Your doubts certainly illustrate the challenges that anyone would face who'd oversee the creation of a national museum in Spain.

Basically, before anything can happen in that direction, I think there must be much more experimentation. It's probably best to start off with a whole series of temporary exhibits before even beginning the discussion about a national museum. Here, it's actually helpful that Spain is organized into seventeen autonomous communities. After the Law of Historical Memory of 2007, those communities started making their own laws, which often go much further than the national law did. At one point, you even saw them competing with each other. The new progressive government in Madrid will likely be able to learn from those regional experiences as it prepares to update the national law.

15

Ricard Vinyes

"Spanish Liberals Have Always Been
More Spanish Than Liberal. It's Been the
Bane of Our Existence."

Ricard Vinyes is an unusual historian. Unlike some of his academic colleagues in Spain, he's not been bothered by the grassroots call for a different kind of history. In fact, he celebrates the involvement of regular citizens in broad debates about the past and its meaning for the present. He also believes that it's the job of the state to make those debates possible, even if they lead to clashes between narratives. Memory, after all, like politics, is conflict. And it's up to the democratic state to allow for and manage that conflict.

Vinyes, for that matter, holds some controversial positions of his own. He categorically rejects the common notion that we have a *duty* to remember, for example. For him, memory is less a duty than a civil right. Any citizen who wishes to should be able to help give shape to the narrative of the collective past; but no one should be forced to participate. For this reason, he is also opposed to the adoption of laws meant to either impose or prohibit certain narratives of the past (Vinyes 2009).

Born in Barcelona in 1952, Vinyes holds a professorship in contemporary history at the University of Barcelona, where his research has focused on twentieth-century Spain, Catalonia, and Europe. In 2002, he revealed how the dictatorship systematically separated imprisoned women from their children, a dramatic story that formed the basis for the groundbreaking book *Irredentas: Las presas políticas y sus hijos en las cárceles franquistas* (2002; Unredeemed: Woman political prisoners and their children in Francoist prisons), which inspired the documentary *Els nens perduts del franquisme* (Armengou and Belis, dirs., 2002; The lost children of Francoism). In recent years, he's held important administrative positions in the regional government of Catalonia and the city government of Barcelona, where he has developed innovative programming on topics of democratic memory. Ten years ago, he was appointed to the commission charged with rethinking the Valley of the Fallen, which first recommended the removal of Franco's remains. I spoke with him in January 2020.

———

Two recurring motifs in the grassroots movement for the recovery of historical memory have been the call for a truth commission—an idea also pushed by representatives of the United Nations—and a national museum of the Civil War and Francoism. You are skeptical on both counts.

I'm not just skeptical, but openly critical. There is no doubt in my mind that both ideas are misguided.

Why is a truth commission a bad idea?

First off, we should remember that truth commissions have historically accompanied transitions to democracy. This is true for Latin America, but also, for example, for Germany after the unification. In Spain, the transition happened more than forty years ago. At this point, there's little a commission could do that hasn't already been accomplished. What truth is there really left to discover? We pretty much know everything there is to know about the war and the dictatorship—or, in any case, historians have uncovered much more information by now, and in empirically more sound ways, than any of the most well-known truth commissions, like those of Chile, Argentina, or Peru, were able to.

To be sure, in Spain there have been serious issues with bringing historians' work to a larger audience. But that is due to a different problem: there simply hasn't been a proper public policy around questions of memory. The state has not addressed the need to transmit more broadly the knowledge about the past produced by historians and other scholars. When Garzón opened his case in 2008, for example, he was surprised to hear about the child deportations that took place between 1938 and 1948, when that information was already known.

Why, then, do the Special Rapporteurs of the United Nations, or even politicians like Pedro Sánchez, insist on the need for a truth commission?

In my opinion, the UN Rapporteurs don't understand the situation fully. I see them as part of the *gentry* of memory management. As far as Spanish politicians are concerned, I've come to realize that if they call for a truth commission it's out of pure mental laziness. They simply don't know what else to come up with. Latin America is invoked as a model, but that's often based on a misunderstanding of the reality on the ground. An important demand in Spain, for instance, is to annul the amnesty law to clear the way for the judicial prosecution of members of the regime. But in Latin America, truth commissions were often designed precisely in order to *prevent* such prosecution. In practice, they often functioned as a full-stop law—at least from the government standpoint.

Politicians also hope that a truth commission will be able to establish a unified narrative about the war and the dictatorship. And that's something I strongly oppose as well, for the same reason that I oppose legislation on issues of memory. We cannot follow the French model. The idea that the state should adopt a particular interpretation of the past and throw its full weight behind it is simply unacceptable. In my view, it's the job of the state to make possible and manage a public memory *policy*, but never to impose a public memory. More importantly, the French laws have been a clear failure. Take the Loi Gayssot from 1990, which condemns Holocaust denial. To be sure, over the years we've fortunately seen the development of many outstanding cultural programs about the Holocaust. There are a great number of good books on the topic, too, both scholarly and for the larger public. And yet, despite all that, there are still people who insist on denying that the Holocaust happened. If only it were possible to solve that question through legislation! But we must accept that it isn't. In practice, the problem has much deeper roots that depend on cultural contexts and conjunctures. There is no simple solution, least of all legislative.

You said that, in France, much good work has been done around Holocaust education. The same is not true for Spain when it comes to the war and the dictatorship.

I am very concerned about education. There's a serious gap between the wealth of scholarly work done and the poverty of the current curricular content. One of the problems I faced when I worked in the city government of Barcelona was that the city doesn't control educational policy; that's in the regional government's remit. Still, what's key in education is *how* things are transmitted, through what kinds of structures. Imposing established narratives is something to be avoided at all times. Rather than spending resources on a useless truth commission whose only purpose is for politicians to congratulate themselves, we should be spending money on designing sound public memory policies and sound structures for transmission.

How about the idea of a national museum of the Civil War and Francoism?

Once again, my first questions would be: Why this insistence? To what end? Of course, the word *museum* carries a great amount of prestige in Western societies. If you look at France, you see how, after World War II, the first thing resistance groups do is request that city governments create museums. Now in France, museums have a Napoleonic grandeur they lack in Spain. If your experience is enshrined in a French museum, it becomes glorious—in this case, the glory of the antifascist struggle against the Nazis. But, to go back to Spain, why would Spain want or need a museum of the Civil War and dictatorship? The cliché reply would be: "Because knowledge serves as protection; a country that doesn't know its past is condemned to repeat it," and so forth. That, of course, is a misunderstanding. Knowledge of the past can help us develop criteria by which to assess the present. But it does not protect us against repetition. A museum, moreover, is defined by its collection. That's a major difficulty right there: what collection would a museum like this have? Then there's the question of the permanent exhibition, which would be an established, fixed narrative. That's another huge problem. Who's going to be creating it? Don't forget that it's Spain we're talking about, not Sweden.

To summarize your position: a national museum of the Civil War and Francoism is neither desirable nor feasible.

Again, I think that what we're dealing with here is a form of laziness. When people don't know what to do, they propose to create a museum.

I understand your hesitance about imposing top-down, unified narratives about the past. But isn't that exactly what history textbooks tend to do?

Sure, but textbooks are not commissioned by the central state. In Spain, every autonomous community controls its own educational policy, sometimes exclusively so. This automatically means the discourse about the past is more polycentric. Which to me is just fine; war, after all, is always experienced locally. More importantly, while education is regulated, it's so only through broad guidelines. The narrative expressed in a museum's collection and permanent exhibit is much more specific.

You have long denounced the passivity of the Spanish state when it comes to memory policy. Ever since the Transition, you've written, there has been a huge vacuum in this area. If a truth commission or museum are not the right way to fill this vacuum, what is?

There's a lot the state can do. It can take measures to promote academic research on the past and make sure that the results of that research end up in the school curriculum. And when I say research, I am not just referring to historians, but also to art and to fields like anthropology, which generate kinds of knowledge that go beyond the conventional museum. The state could also have a permanent policy in place to support temporary exhibitions, invite artists in residence, and so forth. In Spain, at the level of the central state this route has been all but unexplored. But it's a good one. It's certainly the direction we've taken in Barcelona, where we've been able to do a lot of good work, including at the neighborhood level. Where the state should step in, too, is in the matter of the mass graves. The administration's passivity in that area is beyond shameful and entirely unjustified. Frankly, it's been a disaster, when it's such an easy problem to solve. The state should take charge of those exhumations once and for all.

Ricard Vinyes

The Left in Spain has increasingly blamed the Transition for the country's current problems. As a result, the call for a "second Transition" has been growing stronger.

A transition toward what exactly? To be honest, I am not at all sure a second Transition would be a good idea, especially not given the current state of things. I mean, revising the Constitution now? What kind of new constitution would we end up with? It scares me even to imagine it. But you are right that the Transition has become a principle of causal determination. By now, the Transition is invoked to explain the past, the present, and the future. That is not a good thing. But the process by which it has come to assume this central hermeneutic role can be described in historicist, cultural, and political terms.

Can you elaborate?

Remember that, in administrative terms, the model of the Spanish Transition is created after the Socialists win their first absolute majority, in 1982. According to the Socialists' narrative, the Transition is the be-all end-all. There is no life beyond it: it was fantastic, wonderful, a miracle, and so forth. Of course, that narrative was annoying as hell. My generation of historians, who presented our doctoral dissertations in the 1980s, vigorously argued against it, showing that the Transition had been far from exemplary. We did, however, accept that the Transition had been driven by the desire to block the continuity of the dictatorship, and we agreed that it had succeeded in that effort, albeit through a series of pacts with the regime. We acknowledged that the armed forces had watched the whole process with suspicion, which is reflected in some parts of the Constitution. But—and this is important—we also acknowledged that the Transition took place in a context in which the Left wielded a powerful cultural hegemony. And that fact, too, is reflected in the Constitution.

The debate about the Transition continues throughout the 1980s. But then, in the '90s, those of us who had been critical of the exemplarity of the process suddenly found ourselves faced with two new, unexpected fronts, one on the Left and one on the Right, both equally harmful. The narrative that emerged on the Left, or appeared to come from the Left, said: "Not only was the Transition not exemplary; it was, in fact, a scam, because the Left played no role in it." At that moment, the Transition turns into a principle of causal determination *as a reaction* to the Socialist narrative. While the Socialist narrative maintained that all was wonderful thanks to an exemplary Transition, some on the Left now claimed that all would have been better if the Transition would have been different. This narrative is still gaining strength today.

What was the new front on the Right? I assume you're thinking of authors like Pío Moa and César Vidal, non-academics whose bestselling books about the Second Republic and the Civil War revived the basic elements of Franco's version of Spanish history by blaming the Republic for the war and presenting Franco as a national savior.

That's right. In 1996, after fourteen years of Socialist governments, José María Aznar takes over as prime minister. Now, Aznar was a very talented politician. He was the first political leader who managed to unite a Spanish Right that had been atomized since the nineteenth century. And in addition to uniting it, he gave it a cultural and political discourse. With regard to the Transition, Aznar's contribution was key. The Socialists' narrative of the past was based on the idea that "we were all to blame" for what happened during the Civil War. Which is the message against which my generation riled up. But then Pío Moa appeared, who told the Left, "It's not true we were all to blame. The only ones who carry blame are you." This was an incredibly important novelty. For the first time since Franco's death, the Right shook off its complexes. The amount of support that Moa received from Aznar and his think tank, the FAES, was extraordinary. When journalists asked Aznar what he was planning to read over the summer, he replied, "Pío Moa." Moa received an enormous amount of PR, was interviewed on national television, and so forth. Now, the polarization that Moa and Aznar generated further radicalized the other position, which maintained that the Transition was a disaster and is the explanation for every problem we have today. All of which brings us to our current mess.

I sense a kind of fatalism in the idea that the Transition is the root of all evil. Could this be a legacy of Francoism, an upside-down version Franco's grandiose exceptionalism?

In fact, it goes back further than that. Sometimes it seems that Francoism appeared out of nowhere. But it inherited all the currents of Spain's most conservative and reactionary thought. Thanks to the dictatorship, those currents run all the way through the '40s, '50s, '60s, and '70s, right up to our present day. They continue to shape the thought of more than one Spanish liberal, and can even be detected in some intellectuals in the Socialist Party.

Can you give an example?

Take October 12, the *Fiesta de la Raza*. That holiday was invented in the years of the Second Republic. As it turns out, the Republicans, too, loved the idea of *Hispanidad*, the notion of a transatlantic Spanish-speaking community tied together by language and culture. Despite the fact that *Hispanidad* was also one of the banners of the Far Right, Manuel Azaña and company championed the idea and decided to declare October 12, the day that celebrates Columbus, to be the national holiday, and not, for example, April 14, the day the Second Republic was proclaimed. A big mistake, because with this move they basically threw the game to the Right. But then again, Spanish liberals have always been more Spanish than liberal. It's been the bane of our existence.

Which also explains why Spanish liberalism is no stranger to feelings of imperial nostalgia.

Indeed. But get this: in 1986, the Socialists, who by then had governed the country with an absolute majority for four years, had a tremendous opportunity to make a clean break and separate the celebration of the nation from the celebration of empire. They had the chance to pick a different day. March 19, the day Spain's first liberal constitution was adopted, would have been an option. Or April 14. There were plenty of other candidates, and as every politician knows in those situations, if you don't find a good date, you simply invent one. But what did the Socialists do? They decided, once again, to have the national holiday coincide with *Hispanidad*, the Día de la Raza. What a lost opportunity, at the hand of politicians, no less, who think of themselves as internationalists and who don't tire of criticizing nationalism.

Elsewhere you have argued that, in democratic Spain, the desire to avoid ideological conflict makes politicians turn to patriotism as the melting pot in which those ideological conflicts can be dissolved.

Interestingly, we are seeing the same thing happening in Europe. Take the House of European History in Brussels, a museum built to celebrate European identity. That, too, is meant to dissolve the continent's many conflictive histories, by constructing Europe as if it were a nation-state. It's bad news. And it doesn't work.

What's interesting to me is that the architects of the project don't make any effort to hide this element of social engineering. They're completely open about the artificiality of the operation.

And ironically, they all claim to be anti-nationalists—and then they accuse us of nationalism! [*Laughs.*]

Speaking of social engineering, you served on the blue-ribbon commission on the Valley of the Fallen, whose 2011 report recommended that Franco's remains be moved—which finally happened eight years later.

Yes, the commission. I remember those debates well. Before we began our work, we met with Ramón Jáuregui, who then served in Prime Minister Zapatero's cabinet. "The mandate," Jáuregui told us, "is to create a space for the reconciliation of all Spaniards." I immediately spoke up, and two others joined me. "Dear Minister," I said, "I understand the mandate perfectly, and I respect it. But let me say this. Reconciliation in Spain has already taken place. It occurred during the Transition. As long, that is, as we understand reconciliation in institutional terms and not on an interpersonal level, which is not a level that the administration should concern itself with. This institutional reconciliation was embodied in the Parliament and the Constitution, and in people's willingness to accept all the rules of the democratic game. That's done and over with." This got us into a huge debate and we finally agreed to respect our disagreements.

What do you think the central government should do with the Valley of the Fallen now that Franco is gone? After all, it's still a national monument.

The physical structure is in terrible shape and has been for a long time, despite the money spent to repair it. As I wrote around the time of the exhumation, I think the government should not try to turn the Valley into anything else, least of all a center for reconciliation. Rather, it should allow the monument to fall into ruin, which in fact is one of the options included in our final report. In a state of collapse— which it is on the cusp of, anyway—the Valley would be a great teaching tool. It'd illustrate the ethical, political, and religious collapse of what it was built to extol.

16

Emilio Silva

*"The Transition Imposed a
Monotheistic Narrative"*

Emilio Silva is a writer, journalist, and citizen activist who
has spent the last twenty years of his life fighting for the
"recovery of historical memory"—a shorthand phrase for
the multiple demands of the grassroots movement that
Silva helped create as co-founder of the Association for
the Recovery of Historical Memory (ARMH in its Spanish
acronym). Among the achievements the movement can be
credited with are the adoption of the 2007 Memory Law,
the by now broadly accepted designation of the victims of
Francoism as "disappeared," and the exhumation of the
former dictator's remains from the Valley of the Fallen.

Silva, who was born in Navarra in 1965, lives and works
in Madrid. A widely published author and influential public
intellectual, he is something of a living legend—although, like
many Spaniards, he depends for his subsistence on freelance
gigs and short-term contracts, interspersed with regular stints

of unemployment. But whether he's formally employed or not, the shenanigans of Spain's political class are keeping him busy. I interviewed him in late February 2020. A week before, the conservative city government of Madrid had decided to eliminate the plaque with twelve lines of verse by the poet Miguel Hernández, who died in a Francoist prison shortly after the war, from a public monument at the capital's Almudena Cemetery. A couple of months earlier, the city had instructed the removal, from the same monument, of the stone tiles inscribed with the names of close to three thousand *madrileños* executed by the regime. In both cases, Silva's organization took the lead in a vigorous protest campaign.

Ignacio Echevarría has argued that the holdovers from Francoism are no longer a major problem for Spanish society. Claiming that they are—or misrecognizing certain traits of the political Right as Francoist—is a grave political mistake, he said. In fact, he wrote, the features that part of the Left sees as Francoist are much older, and in part quite new. Does that position contradict what you have written about the continued presence of sociological Francoism in all spheres of Spanish society?

Evidently, many of Spain's problems go much farther back than the dictatorship. But the current source of those problems— the elements that still today are blocking the true modernization of Spanish society—are the legacies of Francoism. Echevarría is right to warn against concentrating the blame on the figure of Franco. Francoism has developed into a complex system of social relations, a whole social and economic structure, that is still in force today.

What has allowed it to survive?

Among other things, the fact that the Spanish governments from the end of the dictatorship until the present, independent of the political party in charge, have for the most part consisted of descendants of the Franco regime. It is these children of Francoism who have set clear limits to the modernization of Spanish society. For example, they've allowed the Catholic Church to maintain an extraordinary amount of power over the educational system—manifested, among other things, in the marginalization of philosophy courses in secondary schools. They've also allowed corporations that flourished under Francoism and its use of slave labor to maintain their economic power and corrupting influence.

Have those limits also affected academic research?

Absolutely. Just look at the regional government of Madrid. Here we are, in the year 2020, in a region that holds 179 municipalities and boasts a set of great public universities. Yet there isn't the slightest interest in developing a research program to investigate the history of Francoist repression in this area.

So Echevarría doesn't quite get it right.

The argument he is trying to make about the civil war as a "mythical substrate" in a way misses the point. The problem is not the war. It's the dictatorship: the almost forty years of so-called peace during which Francoism imposed its infrastructure, its ideology of national-Catholicism, and its entire social and economic project, while blocking any and all alternatives.

The United Nations has called for a Spanish Truth Commission. This proposal has been met with skepticism. Ricard Vinyes, for example, believes it'd be useless.

Truth commissions elsewhere have helped clear the way for reparations for victims—something that hasn't happened in Spain, despite the many years that have gone by since the Transition. They've also helped address human rights violations, another important area that in Spain remains completely unaddressed. I'm not sure we need a Truth Commission per se, but we do need something. I think we need some kind of official report that focuses not on victims—who have been the focus of the entire debate in Spain so far—but on the perpetrators. We need to know once and for all who they were and what they did.

Do you see the current government making progress in this area?

So far, it doesn't look like it. For example, the government has proposed a couple of new commemorative holidays that pretend to mark a change but in fact continue to mask the reality of the repression. For commemorating the Spanish victims of Nazism, for instance, the government has proposed May 5, the anniversary of the liberation of Europe in 1945. This makes very little sense in the Spanish context. That liberation, after all, passed Spain by: we suffered under a fascist dictatorship for an additional thirty years. Even the surviving Spanish Republicans who were freed from the

Nazi camps were not liberated fully, because they could not return to their homeland. Most of them died in exile. Another proposal is to make October 31 a holiday to commemorate the victims of Francoism. Why October 31? Because it marks the day that the Spanish parliament approved the democratic Constitution of 1978.

Now when you think about it, both of these two dates help to blur the repressive reality of the dictatorship. I'd argue they reflect the level of protection that the Spanish state is still willing to provide to the perpetrators. The same is true of the government's extreme reluctance when it comes to declassifying the personnel records of police officers, some of whom are still alive, who tortured dozens of citizens but who continue to enjoy state pensions and were never even obliged to return the medals they earned serving the Francoist state. There clearly is a great fear that releasing those records will set a precedent for exposing other former officials. So while it is true that, by now, we have a lot of information about the victims, we lack all kinds of knowledge when it comes to the victimizers: who they were, what they did, how they benefited.

When I interviewed you four years ago, you said that Spain's dominant perception of Francoism had shifted, thanks in large part to the hundreds of exhumations of mass graves organized by the ARMH and similar organizations—and despite the largely passive stance of the Spanish state. As an activist and family member of victims of rightwing repression, what do you still demand of the state at this point?

In a way, the dictatorship and the Transition combined to form the perfect crime. The political parties that were

legalized after Franco's death gave up their right to denounce
crimes from the past. They distanced themselves from the
Second Republic. They allowed those who were responsible for human rights violations to continue their political
careers as if nothing had happened. Meanwhile, the victims
kept their silence, a silence induced by fear. After the failed
coup of February 1981, this fear-induced silence became
the new social consensus. Our activism around historical
memory broke this consensus. What helped introduce this
shift was the appearance of the victims' bodies in the mass
graves we were exhuming, and the shocking images that
these exhumations produced.

And yet impunity still reigns.

Here, the state has been completely complicit. In fact, it
continues to take advantage of that impunity. It's forsak-
ing its duties. What it should do, first, is to guarantee the
rights of the victims and, second, open its basements once
and for all, making all the documentation that has not been
destroyed available for research and consultation. That'd allow us to finally document the horrors of Francoism and
uncover the many, many things we don't yet know.

Although much research has been done over the years.

It's sometimes suggested that we know pretty much everything there is to know about the dictatorship. That's not
true. A second problem is the dissemination of the knowledge that we do have. In that sense, the state's protection
of the perpetrators has extended into secondary education,

where the dictatorship is barely covered in the curriculum—
and if it is, it's covered badly.

In addition to the mass declassification of archives and a serious re-
form of history education, what else should the state do?

It should clear the way for court action by judicially
acknowledging the crimes of the dictatorship as crimes,
rather than as unfortunate historical realities. Because the
victims of those crimes are still here among us. The concept of impunity, moreover, is not just applicable in a judicial sense. It covers a whole range of dimensions. In Spain,
impunity has reigned in documentary terms, in informa-
tional terms, but also in relation to education, the university system, and the media.

The current government has proposed making extolling Franco and
the dictatorship punishable by law. The reception has been mixed,
even on the Left.

I share some people's doubts about restricting freedom of
expression. A bigger problem is that the government seems
to want to declare extolling Francoism a crime without first
branding the crimes of the dictatorship as crimes. How can
you maintain that it's not a crime to perpetrate more than a
hundred thousand forced disappearances, but it *is* a crime
to celebrate those responsible for that repression? If what
we are seeking is guarantees of nonrepetition, making the
apology of Francoism illegal is going to be much less effective than working to include democratic values into our
primary and secondary school curriculum.

The deficits in that area are pretty clear.

Young people today who yell "¡*Viva Franco!*" or have "Cara al sol," the Falangist anthem, as their cellphone ringtone, have often no real idea who Franco was. But so far, I have heard no government commit to that kind of educational project.

Will or should there ever be a national museum of the Civil War and Francoism?

About fifteen years ago, I was interviewed by someone affiliated with a US company that specialized in historical monuments and museums. They had worked on the Holocaust Museum in Washington, DC, and had come to Spain to study the possibility of a museum on the Civil War and Francoism. After we had coffee together, they said their next appointments were with political representatives. "I'm sorry to tell you," I said, "that you've come many decades too early. It'll be a long time before any Spanish politician will be able to put their weight behind a project like that."

It seems you were right.

Let me give you an example. Madrid has a museum of the city. Visitors see the city's whole history, from the first human settlements to Madrid's designation as the national capital and the urban development of the nineteenth and early twentieth centuries. But once we get to the late 1920s, the narrative stops dead in its tracks. Not one of the city governments we've had has been willing to tell what happened in the 1930s, during the years of the Second Republic and the war. This doesn't just show a lack of political will. It shows the administration's *inability* to narrate this historical period.

But wouldn't it be good to have a museum?

Yes, of course I wish there were a museum of the horrors of Francoism. Just like I wish we really had the chance to turn the Valley of the Fallen into an educational space that could tell about the role Catholicism played in the persecution of its dissidents—something that the history of the monument's construction illustrates very well.

But you don't see it happening anytime soon.

Given Spain's political reality, given the state's willingness to protect the perpetrators' impunity, it will be very hard to create a museum with the narrative clarity we'd need. That said, there has been some movement. The fact that the Partido Popular's right wing has split off to form Vox, for example, has allowed for the return of the terms *fascist* and *fascism*, which were long considered improper in referring to the Spanish Right. Perhaps we're entering a new political reality in which a democratic consensus is allowed to emerge that agrees to condemn the Far Right in the context of its international rise. That consensus is sorely needed— but also, I fear, very unlikely.

The Transition implied a certain attitude toward the twentieth-century past. Do you think that solving Spain's challenges today will require a redefinition of that attitude—that is, a second Transition?

Or is the focus on the past really a distraction from much more urgent problems?

It's more than a mere distraction. What we're talking about, after all, is what kind of country we, as citizens, want to build together. We're talking about rights. The Transition imposed a single narrative of our past, a monotheistic narrative so to speak.

Monotheistic?

I use that term because the single narrative of the Transition has a lot to do with the culture of Catholicism—which in Spain has been much more of an ideology than a religious practice. Catholicism, in Spain, has been about the exercise of power.

What kind of narrative can take its place?

What Spain needs is a narrative that allows it to understand what the Second Republic was. Or, simply, what a republic can be. There are many people who reject the monarchy but have little idea about its alternatives. Some are afraid of a republic because it has been associated for so many years with notions of chaos—a narrative instituted by Francoism that the Transition perpetuated.

I believe the problem of memory in Spain is central. Being able to debate the past, to reflect on it, to take a position in relation to it, is key. But as long as the criminal nature of the dictatorship is denied or hidden in school curricula, government discourse, and the media, that debate will be rigged. The elites who had strong ties to Francoism and who continue to wield power in the social and economic structures that were built during the Franco years are playing with a marked deck of cards.

Look, I read a lot about these things and consider myself reasonably well informed. And yet, when I read Antonio Maestre's book about the economic legacies of Francoism, I was horrified to discover to what extent the tentacles of Francoism reach into every single part of our society today. If we think of Spain as a tree whose roots reach into the soil of history, it's clear that we are not drinking from the Second Republic or other progressive periods. The subsoil that feeds us is still drenched in Francoism.

CONCLUSION
Not So Different After All

"Anywhere else, the information about the scheme . . . would have cost the prime minister his job. In Spain, it only sped up the fall of the editors who'd dared publish it," David Jiménez, the former editor of *El Mundo*, wrote when describing his paper's publication of the Partido Popular's shadow books—showing, among other things, years' worth of corporate kickbacks and under-the-table payments to party execs (2019, chapter 4). Elsewhere in his memoir, Jiménez talks about corporate bribes for journalists, sighing, "What would have been unacceptable in countries with a long tradition of press freedom was considered normal in [Spain]" (chapter 9). In January 2020, the journalist Rosa María Artal wrote that the trial of those held responsible for the Catalan referendum for independence was a judicial scandal to which "a serious and mature country" would have reacted with a thorough investigation (Artal 2020). One of the people on trial, the Catalan Left Republican leader Oriol Junqueras, remarked in an interview in the same month that "a normal country wouldn't have had a problem" with the referendum (Pérez 2020).

Anyone who follows the Spanish news recognizes these arguments. Spaniards who are critical of their country have a standard rhetorical move: our country is different; things that don't work right in Spain operate better elsewhere. The grass is generally seen to be greener in northwestern Europe and, sometimes, the United States. This tendency is not exclusive to Spain, of course. The Left in the United States, for example, has resorted to it for years to bolster its arguments in favor of gun control, universal healthcare, or prison reform. As Bernie Sanders likes to say, "We are the only major country on Earth that doesn't guarantee health care to all people as a right" (Greenberg 2015). Bryan Stevenson has long called attention to the unacceptable racial bias in the US judicial system by arguing that Germany would never accept a situation in which its courts would disproportionally target Jews for the death penalty.

Still, in Spain the tactic has been particularly prevalent—and particularly effective. For the memory movement these past twenty years, comparing Spain to Germany or the Southern Cone helped call attention to Spain's lack of concern for transitional justice and victims' rights. In a 2003 documentary about the first exhumations of mass graves from the Civil War, an indignant woman states:

> I hear no one saying that we should forget the Holocaust, that we should forget the death train that went to Auschwitz, that we should forget those who Pinochet eliminated in one way or another. And yet in Spain we had to draw a veil, forget all our family members, forget the suffering, the fears, and everything else. Here, I

don't know why, we must forget everything—wipe the slate clean! (Armengou and Belis 2003)

When I spoke with the journalist Miguel de Lucas in 2019, he recalled an intervention from Angela Merkel, Germany's chancellor, that had taken place in early December of that year. While visiting Auschwitz, she'd underscored the importance of preserving the camp for future generations to see. She'd also said that "Remembering the crimes . . . is a responsibility which never ends. It belongs inseparably to our country" (BBC 2019). "Merkel is the leader of a classic conservative party," de Lucas told me. "Now think about it: What would need to happen, how much time would need to pass, for a leader of a Spanish party on the Right to make a similar statement? Not only would it be unthinkable that the Right would say anything remotely similar; it'd even be hard to find it coming from the Spanish Left."

There are clear advantages to this type of argument, which has been particularly popular on the Spanish Left. It plays on the public's patriotic pride by activating a reaction of shame. It also connects with two long-dominant motifs in Spaniards' self-perception: on the one hand, the aspiration to European "normality" (Delgado 2014) and, on the other, the awareness of persistent difference, a difference explained as *abnormality* and often read as a lack: a lack of maturity, a lack of accountability, a lack of democratic tradition (Artal 2020; Jiménez 2019).

Yet beyond its obvious rhetorical effectiveness, the tactic has downsides as well. For one, by exaggerating Spain's difference and other countries' presumed normality, it runs the risk of fatalism: the assumption that the democratic or cultural "health" or "maturity" that seems to be the norm elsewhere will always be out of Spaniards' reach. (In practice, of course, no other country is quite as "normal" as it may appear to envious eyes from abroad.) Secondly, the tactic risks de-emphasizing the extent to which countries share similar challenges. When it comes to determining what to do with a complicated, conflicted, or violent past, after all, Spain is far from alone in the world. I just mentioned Bryan Stevenson, who has argued for the past thirty years that the United States has never properly come to terms with its history of racial violence and the persistent effects of that violence in the present. Few things illustrate this point better than the persistence, and recent rise, of white supremacism. The Netherlands, my own country, is only now beginning to face up to its historical role in the trans-Atlantic slave trade and the violence it inflicted on its colonial populations, particularly during Indonesia's struggle for independence. Even Germany—often cited as a positive example by Stevenson and the Spanish memory movement—has its problems, as the rise of Alternative für Deutschland (AfD) shows. "If the French are rightly proud of their emperor and the Britons of Nelson and Churchill, we have the right to be proud of the achievements of the German soldiers in two world wars," said Alexander Gauland, an AfD candidate, at a campaign meeting in September 2017. Earlier in 2017, Björn Höcke, a state deputy for the AfD in the former East Germany, criticized the Holocaust Memorial in Berlin as a "monument of shame," calling for a radically different approach to the way Germans relate to the Nazi past ("AfD Co-Founder Says" 2017).

The proud invocation of a heroic past has been a key element in Far-Right discourse across the world. Rejecting self-critical readings of national history, Far-Right parties claim the people's right to an uncomplicated form of patriotic pride, rejecting any form of national shame or embarrassment as unnecessary and weakening impositions from the Left. In October 2018, Santiago Abascal, the leader of Spain's young Far-Right party Vox, claimed before thousands of supporters that Spaniards "have more right than anyone to call ourselves European": "After all, we saved Europe from the Muslim onslaught during our 700-year Reconquest!" (Vox España 2018). "History matters, it matters a lot," Abascal told reporters half a year later at the Holy Cave of Covadonga, a Catholic sanctuary in the Picos de Europa region of Asturias where, according to legend, a small band of Christian warriors led by Don Pelayo—and assisted by the Virgin Mary—defeated a Muslim army in a mythical, early eighth-century battle that gave the starting shot for the *Reconquista* for Christendom of a Muslim-dominated Iberia (Vanguardia 2019b). "And we are not the least bit ashamed to celebrate what our forefathers did over the centuries. . . . We will never apologize for their deeds. Rather, we hold them up as a guide: a guide for battle, for resistance, and for a set of normal values rooted in the common sense that we were taught in our homes" (Ruptly 2019).

In the Netherlands, the Far-Right Forum for Democracy (FvD), led by the photogenic young politician Thierry Baudet, has picked similar local and national battles in the name of the defense of freedom and patriotism. When, in the fall of 2019, the Amsterdam Museum announced that it would stop referring to the seventeenth century as the "Golden Age," Baudet joined the public debate defending the traditional term. In September 2019, the FvD premiered a series of short online documentaries featuring the party leader himself as an impromptu history teacher. "The image of our past that we've been taught is distorted," he said in the first video. "We've been made to feel ashamed and guilty, but there is no reason for that. The people who made the Netherlands in many cases did wonderful things. They are a source of inspiration and pride" (Forum voor Democratie 2019a). One of the first episodes celebrated Admiral Michiel de Ruyter (1607–1676), who led the Dutch Navy against the English and French, as "the greatest patriot of all times" (Forum voor Democratie 2019b). "We have to learn to love our country again," said the online presentation of the series on the party's website, "We must dare to be proud once more of who we are": "We're putting a stop to . . . the shame and apologies. We love our heroes!" (Forum voor Democratie 2019a). In the United States, the 1776 Commission appointed by President Trump wrote, "it is our mission . . . to restore our national unity by rekindling a brave and honest love for our country," and "we must stand up to the petty tyrants in every sphere who demand that we speak only of America's sins while denying her greatness" (President's Advisory 1776 Commission, 16).

As they seek to redefine the narrative of national history along patriotic lines, Europe's and America's right-wing populists leave little doubt about whom they are up against. They explicitly impugn the two principal institutional sources of authoritative accounts of the past: the state and the university. In the Netherlands, the FvD has criticized the educational system as a source of "left-wing indoctrination" and called for a central office where students can report biased teachers (Univers 2019), much like, back in 2006, David Horowitz sought to "blow the cover" on academics suspected of promoting anti-American values and to denounce the indoctrination of US students by an overly politicized professoriate.

If I mention these examples, it's to emphasize the commonalities that bind Spain to the rest of the world. Naturally, the German AfD, the Dutch FvD, and the American Far Right are all shaped by their national circumstances, as is Vox in Spain. But that doesn't mean that citizens concerned about these growing movements cannot learn from each other. The same is true for activists, scholars, and policy makers who engage with the difficult work of historical justice, including the thorny issue of reparations, be they of a moral or economic kind. Or for everyone who works to meaningfully incorporate difficult stories from a community's collective past into high-school curricula, museums, monuments, or other sites of memory. Spain may well need a second Transition, whatever shape that process might take—but so do many other countries.

The questions that face Spain now that Franco's body has been reburied, in other words, are not exclusive to Spain. What's the proper way to teach a community's history of violence? How should a state respond to victims' demands for justice and reparation? What is the role of international actors, from the United Nations and Amnesty International to NGOs specializing in mechanisms of transitional justice? What is the moral and material responsibility of groups and individuals whose current privilege can be traced back to past forms of violence and injustice? What does reconciliation look like? Is "coming to terms with the past" a process that ever really ends, or does it start anew for every generation? And perhaps the most crucial question of all: what *is* the role of history in a political practice necessarily preoccupied with the present and future? As we tackle the most urgent challenges of our time, how important is it for us to first, or simultaneously, consider the way we choose to tell and remember—or silence and forget—the past? To close this short book, I'd like to return to my interlocutors in Spain, inviting you now to read their reflections in this broader, global framework.

"The Transition, to me, is like a forty-year old dress that stopped looking good a while ago," Montse Armengou, the filmmaker, told me. "Maybe we gained weight or maybe we lost it; but in any case, as we have gotten older, our taste and needs have changed. Spanish society has matured. In fact, it's matured much more than the entities that govern us. Looking back, it's clear that the Transition was a patch. A temporary solution. It may have worked then—but it definitely no longer does now."

"Speaking in general terms, we could say that for Spanish society—for Spanish democracy—the past is absent," the historian Jaume Claret told me. "In a sense, it simply does not exist. And yet the weight of that absent past is undeniable. On one hand, it's obvious that redefining the relationship with our collective past won't solve any of our current problems in an immediate way. And yet I would argue that dealing with the challenge of the unprocessed past is a *necessary condition* to begin tackling all the other challenges we face. The main problem of the Spanish Right is that it has not been able to rebuild itself on, and connect its electorate with, a genealogy that is not Francoist. But the Left, too, has failed to forge a coherent narrative about the national past."

"Will Spain be able to change its political culture without changing its relationship to the past, or without changing the way it narrates that past from the present?" I asked
the philosopher José Luis Villacañas. "No, it will not," he
replied, adding, "and when I say that, I am referring to
Spanish history in its entirety, not just the Francoist period.
Spain needs to narrate its past differently precisely because
Francoism imposed itself on the whole of it. Without a
new global vision of our own, we won't be able to understand the significance of the Second Republic, for example."
Nor will it be possible to solve the territorial problem, Sebastián Martín, the legal scholar, added. "Take the Catalan
conflict, which is affecting the entire structure of the state.
Any solution will depend directly on how we conceive of
our genealogy as a country. Do we tell a story of a country whose cultural and state unity were in place from the
fifteenth century or even from the time of the Visigoths?
Or is ours a narrative of an irreducible pluralism, made up
of different national sensibilities?"

Manuel Artime is a philosopher who, like Villacañas, has
written extensively on the evolution of Spanish historiography. "Underlying Spain's current political crisis," he told
me, "is a conflict of narratives. On one side are those who
defend Spanish democracy as being spotless and exemplary.
On the other, those who maintain that our democracy is
a crypto-Francoist fiction, an archaic political community
with which we need to break. Stated like that, both positions
are untenable." Underscoring the importance of history for
the political present, Artime pointed to the apparent im-
possibility of Spain's center Left and center Right to form
a coalition government of the type we're used to seeing in

countries like Germany or the Netherlands. "A coalition like that isn't possible in Spain," he said, "because there is no narrative-historical basis for it. There is no common story." While northern Europe built its postwar democracies on the shared account of antifascist resistance, Artime said, Spain did not: "Despite the efforts of many people, a shared narrative of anti-Francoism has yet to emerge. Still, that doesn't mean those efforts have been useless. The mobilizations of the past twenty years have left their trace. It will be hard to put that toothpaste back into the tube."

Meanwhile, the mounting polarization has eroded the viability and legitimacy of parliamentary politics—also a problem not limited to Spain. Here, too, history is a major source of tension. "I sometimes wonder if the Spanish Right is so unwilling to condemn Francoism in clear terms because that means it will have to accept the Second Republic as a historical reference point," Edgar Straehle, a philosopher, told me. "Then again, something similar happens on the opposite side, where the legitimacy of the Republic seems to have been reduced to the fact that it was Franco's enemy. If delegitimating your opponent is your strongest source of legitimacy, then you have a political problem."

Polarization also worries Andreu Navarra, a novelist and cultural historian in Barcelona. In Spain's political landscape, he said, "pluralists, liberals—people who accept the notion of political rivalry while understanding that practicing politics means overcoming conflicts—are fewer and fewer in number. Future historians looking back on this time will conclude that our mentalities have fossilized," he added. "All the Byzantine disputes about the Civil War among people who really have no idea what actually happened only serve to distract from the fact that we are being cheated out of our rights and liberties." Of all my interlocutors, Navarra was the most pessimistic—not only about the possibilities of a second Spanish Transition but about its potential results. "I tend to think of the Constitution of 1978 as a kind of armistice between different versions of Spain that have been unable and unwilling to coexist. Leaving that Constitution behind will lead us into a much more conflictive and violent scenario, given the ultraliberal power dynamics we have already seen put in place in countries like Russia, Turkey, Hungary, or Poland. Spain, I'm afraid, is not headed for improvement. I have very little hope for the future."

"If Spain were able to critically reinterpret its past, the effects would be substantial," the historian Pablo Sánchez León told me. "Still, I am not sure it would provide sufficient clarity to solve the economic, social, or cultural challenges of twenty-first-century Spain. And even for that reinterpretation to take hold, we'd need to account for the high level of compliance among the Spanish population as the country transitioned from dictatorship to democracy. That means we'd have to give up on a double myth: the myth of a mature citizenry that rid itself of the Franco regime through consensus and the myth of the anti-Francoist resistance. Don't get me wrong; letting go of these myths and leaving behind the simplistic conspiracy theories that inform many of the current narratives would be a healthy thing to do for Spanish culture. But even that is no small task."

One place to start is at home, the Seville journalist Miguel de Lucas suggested. Historical memory, collective narratives, always have a personal, affective, and moral dimension. "The other day I was taking a walk in a park close to where I live," he told me. "The park is on the same spot where, for fifty years, the provincial prison stood. When the park was built, the local labor unions insisted that part of the prison be kept intact—the section, precisely, that held political prisoners. I am glad that my son, who is turning one year old this Christmas, will have a park nearby to play in. I'm happy it's a park and not an abandoned prison—or, for that matter, a museum about Franco's repression. And yet I'm also very happy that the prison's façade has remained in place, along with a plaque explaining what once stood there. When my son's a bit older, we can tell him that it was here where the great grandfather of his mother spent several years in prison—not for being a thief or a murderer but because he was the last Republican mayor of a town called Alcalá del Río, and because he was a member of the Socialist Party—a party that shares the name of today's Socialist Party but wasn't quite the same, because in those days, the mayors who belonged to that party got in trouble with the landowners when they took that land to divide it up among poor peasants who often went hungry. 'Your great great grandfather,' we can tell him, 'was liked so much for doing this that the town re-elected him.' Now, of course, telling him this story will not help my son solve any of the problems he might run into as he grows up. He may not even pay that much attention to what we tell him. But some day he might have follow-up questions. And when he does, I'll tell him that he also had a great grandmother, my grandmother, who for years belonged to Franco's women's organization, *la Sección Femenina*. That'll give us a chance to explain to him why his ancestors found themselves on opposite sides, why they ended up in a war with each other, and how come good people ended up in prison without being a thief or a murderer."

ACKNOWLEDGMENTS

This book would not have been possible without the thirty-five individuals, listed below, who generously and patiently responded to my questions; nor would it exist if it had not been for Zack Gresham at Vanderbilt University Press, who first suggested it, and the support of VUP's director, Gianna Mosser, along with the rest of the outstanding staff in Nashville. Among the many friends and colleagues who over the years have helped me think, teach, and write about Spain are Brigitte Adriaensen, Daniel Aguirre Oteiza, Marta Altisent, Palmar Álvarez-Blanco, Manuel Aznar Soler, Robert Bahar, Mari Paz Balibrea, Gonzalo Baptista, David Becerra, Kata Beilin, John Beverley, Carlos Blanco Aguinaga, Harm den Boer, Sara Brenneis, Hans Maarten van den Brink, Miguel Caballero, Peter N. Carroll, Almudena Carracedo, Francie Cate-Arries, Kate Doyle, Simon Doubleday, Cecilia Enjuto-Rangel, Francisco Espinosa Maestre, Carolina Espinoza, James D. Fernández, Teresa Férriz, Michal Friedman, Arjen Fortuin, Joseba Gabilondo, Pedro García-Caro, Pedro García Guirao, Sonia García López, Pablo García

Martínez, Baltasar Garzón, Jorge Gaupp, Anthony Geist, Olga Glondys, François Godicheau, Neil Larsen, Antonio Gómez López-Quiñones, Josh Goode, Ignasi Gozalo-Salellas, Helen Graham, Germán Gullón, Rebecca Haidt, Leslie Harkema, Noemí de Haro, María Hernández-Ojeda, Gina Herrmann, Edgar Illas, Montserrat Iniesta, Jesús Izquierdo Martín, Gabriel Jackson, Ariel Jerez, David Jorge, Dan Kaufman, Paula Kuffer, Jo Labanyi, Germán Labrador, Susan Larson, Fernando Larraz, José Ramón López, Ana Luengo, Enrique Maestu, Steven Marsh, Jonathan Mayhew, Mario Martín Gijón, Cristina Martínez-Carazo, Jordi Marí, Jordi Martí Rueda, Alberto Moreiras, Cristina Moreiras, Luis Moreno-Caballud, Carmen Moreno-Nuño, Gijs Mulder, José María Naharro-Calderón, Robert Newcomb, Anthony Nuckols, Jinke Obbema, Joan Oleza Simó, Azahara Palomeque, Esther Pascua, Óscar Pereira Zazo, Oriol Porta, Paul Preston, Joan Ramon Resina, Aaron Retish, Berta del Río, Jacobo Rivero, Juan Rodríguez, Gayle Rogers, Vicente Rubio-Pueyo, Isis Sadek, Juan Salas, Benita Sampedro, Gervasio Sánchez, Ignacio Sánchez-Cuenca, Antolín Sánchez Cuervo, Ignacio Sánchez-Prado, Yvonne Scholten, Bécquer Seguín, Rosi Song, Sarah Thomas, Steven Torres, Michael Ugarte, Isabelle Touton, Noël Valis, José del Valle, William Viestenz, Teresa Vilarós, Eva Woods Peiró, Cynthia Young, Félix Zamora, and Trisha Ziff. I would also like to thank my students at Oberlin College and my colleagues there: Claire Solomon, Ana María Díaz-Burgos, Sergio Gutiérrez Negrón, Patrick O'Connor, Ana Cara, Jed Deppman, Erik Inglis, Wendy Kozol, Geoff Pingree, Steven Volk, Renee Romano, Patty Tovar, and Kristina Mani. Over the past eight years I have been fortunate to work with outstanding

Spanish, Dutch, and US editors: Alfonso Armada at *FronteraD*; the editorial team at *Contratiempo*; Magda Bandera at *La Marea*; Miguel Mora, Mónica Andrade, and Vanesa Jiménez at *Contexto*; Stephen Twilley at *Public Books*; Roane Carey at *The Nation*; Ricardo Robledo at *Conversación sobre la Historia*; and Rutger van der Hoeven and Xandra Schutte at *De Groene Amsterdammer*. My deepest thanks go to my immediate family—Kim, Jakob, and Maya—for keeping my feet where they belong: on the ground.

INTERVIEWS
AND CORRESPONDENCE

Noelia Adánez, 16 Jan. 2020
Montse Armengou, 24 Dec. 2019
Manuel Artime, 27 Dec. 2019
Magda Bandera, 19 April 2016; 28 Jan. 2020
Mar Cabra, 26 July 2015
David Cabo, 23 July 2015
Alfons Cervera, 30 Jan. 2020
Jaume Claret, 1 Jan. 2020
Trinidad Deiros, 24 July 2015
Cristina Fallarás, 18 Feb. 2020
Jordi Gracia, 21 Dec. 2019
Luis de Guezala, 10 Jan. 2020
Ignacio Echevarría, 19 Jan. 2020
Guillermo Fernández Vázquez, 27 Dec. 2020
Francisco Ferrándiz, 9 Oct. 2019; 24 Jan. 2020
Fernando Hernández Sánchez, 30 Oct. 2019; 10 Jan. 2020
Marije Hristova, 21 Jan. 2020
Enric Juliana, 25 May 2020
Miguel de Lucas, 22 July 2015; 25 Dec. 2019

Antonio Maestre, 12 Feb. 2020

Sebastián Martín, 3 Jan. 2020

Guillem Martínez, 24 July 2015; 14 Feb. 2020

Miguel Mora, 24 July 2015; 8 Jan. 2020

Andreu Navarra, 25 Dec. 2020

Miquel Ramos, 9 Jan. 2020

Manuel Rico, 28 July 2015

Ricardo Robledo, 16 Jan. 2020

Pablo Sánchez León, 19 Jan. 2020

Emilio Silva, 9 Oct. 2019; 27 Feb. 2020

Edgar Straehle, 5 Feb. 2020

Carles Sirera, 2 Jan. 2020

José Luis Villacañas, 8 Jan. 2020

Ricard Vinyes, 22 Jan. 2020

Ángel Viñas, 9 Jan. 2020

José Antonio Zarzalejos, 22 May 2020

BIBLIOGRAPHY

Aduriz, Íñigo. 2020. "El Gobierno arranca con la credibilidad de la política por los suelos: Los expertos culpan al bloqueo y la corrupción." *ElDiario.es*, February 7, 2020. https://www.eldiario.es/politica/principales-problemas-espanoles-institucional-mediaticos_0_993201283.html.

"AfD Co-Founder Says Germans Should Be Proud of Its Second World War Soldiers." 2017. *Guardian*, September 14, 2017. https://www.theguardian.com/world/2017/sep/14/afd-co-founder-alexander-gauland-says-germany-needs-to-reclaim-its-history.

Aguilar, Paloma. 2002. *Memory and Amnesia: The Role of the Spanish Civil War in the Transition to Democracy*. New York: Berghahn.

Aguilar, Paloma, and Leigh A. Payne. 2016. *Revealing New Truths about Spain's Violent Past: Perpetrators' Confessions and Victim Exhumations*. New York: Palgrave.

Álvarez de Toledo, Cayetana. 2020. "Franco, Franco, Franco." *El Mundo*, September 21, 2020. https://www.elmundo.es/opinion/2020/09/21/5f677a37fdddff7c878b4632.html.

Andrés Ibáñez, Perfecto. 2015. *Tercero en discordia: Jurisdicción y juez del Estado constitucional*. Madrid: Trotta.

Aragoneses, Alfons. 2017. "Legal Silences and the Memory of Francoism in Spain." In *Law and Memory: Towards Legal Governance of History*, edited by Uladzislau Belavusau and Aleksandra Gliszczynska-Grabias, 175–94. Cambridge, UK: Cambridge University Press.

Armengou, Montse, and Ricard Belis, dirs. 2002. *Els nens perduts del franquisme*. Barcelona: Televisió de Catalunya.

———. 2003. *Les fosses del silenci*. Barcelona: Televisió de Catalunya.

———. 2013. *Avi, et trauré d'aquí!* Barcelona: Televisió de Catalunya.

Artal, Rosa María. 2020. "Lo que 'sabemos' del acoso que sufrirá el Gobierno." *ElDiario.es*, January 10, 2020. https://www.eldiario.es/zonacritica/sabemos-acoso-informativo-sufrira-gobierno_6_983461664.html.

Baylos Grau, Antonio. 2008. "Derechos económicos e indemnizaciones derivados de la memoria histórica." In *Derecho y memoria histórica*, edited by José Antonio Martín Pallín and Rafael Escudero, 185–208. Madrid: Trotta.

BBC. 2019. "Auschwitz Visit: Angela Merkel Says Germany Must Remember Nazi Crimes." *BBC News*, December 6, 2019. https://www.bbc.com/news/world-europe-50671663.

Bocanegra, Raúl. 2019. "Una jueza defiende al ministro franquista Utrera Molina y condena a Teresa Rodríguez a pagar 5.000 euros a su familia por un tuit." *Público*, May 20, 2019. https://www.publico.es/politica/impunidad-franquismo-jueza-defiende-ministro-franquista-utrera-molina-condena-teresa-rodriguez-pagar-5000-euros-familia-tuit.html.

———. 2020. "La Audiencia de Madrid ratifica la condena a Teresa Rodríguez por un tuit contra el ministro franquista

Utrera Molina." *Público*, November 22, 2020. https://
www.publico.es/politica/audiencia-madrid-ratifica-
condena-teresa-rodriguez-tuit-ministro-franquista-utrera-
molina.html.

Boletín Oficial del Estado. 1982. "Sala Segunda. Recurso de
amparo número 403/81. Sentencia número 2lJ/1982, de 26
de mayo." *Boletín Oficial del Estado* 137, Supplement, 9 June:
19–21.

———. 2007. "LEY 52/2007, de 26 de diciembre, por la que
se reconocen y amplían derechos y se establecen medidas
en favor de quienes padecieron persecución o violencia
durante la guerra civil y la dictadura." *Boletín Oficial
del Estado* 310 (27 de diciembre): 53410–16. http://www.
mpr.es/NR/rdonlyres/D03898BE-21B8-4CB8-BBD1-
D1450E6FD7AD/85567/boememoria.pdf.

Borraz, Marta. 2019. "La Policía multa con la Ley Mordaza a
una activista de Femen por irrumpir en un acto franquista
de Falange en 2018." *ElDiario.es*, October 3, 2019. https://
www.eldiario.es/sociedad/Policia-Ley-Mordaza-Femen-
Falange_0_948755880.html.

Bosch, Joaquim, and Ignacio Escolar. 2018. *El secuestro de la
justicia: Virtudes y problemas del sistema judicial*. Barcelona:
Roca. Kindle.

Caballero, Fátima. 2019. "Ayuso se pregunta 'qué será lo
siguiente' tras la exhumación de Franco: '¿Arderán las
parroquias como en el 36?'" *ElDiario.es*, October 3, 2019.

Carracedo, Almudena, and Robert Bahar, dirs. 2018. *El silencio
de otros*. Madrid: Semilla Verde (*The Silence of Others*, Argot
Pictures [2019]).

Castillo, Gorka. 2020. "Cloacas del Estado: Caso abierto."
CTXT: Revista Contexto, February 15, 2020. https://ctxt.
es/es/20200203/Politica/31003/Gorka-Castillo-cloacas-del-
estado-Villarejo-Unidas-Podemos-policia-patriotica.htm.

Catalán, Agustín. 2015. "Pablo Casado y su resbalón con las fosas." *El Periódico*, June 19, 2015. https://www.elperiodico. com/es/videos/politica/pablo-casado-y-su-resbalon-con-las-fosas/3454499.shtml.

Cebrián, Juan Luis. 2016. *Primera página: Vida de un periodista, 1944–1988*. Madrid: Debate.

Claret Miranda, Jaume. 2006. *El atroz desmoche: La destrucción de la Universidad española por el franquismo, 1936–1945*. Barcelona: Crítica.

Clavero, Bartolomé. 2019. *Constitución a la deriva: Imprudencia de la justicia y otros desafueros*. Barcelona: Pasado y Presente.

Clemente, Enrique. 2007. "¿Por qué voy a tener que condenar yo el franquismo?" *La voz de Galicia*, November 25, 2007. https://www.lavozdegalicia.es/noticia/espana/2007/10/14/ tener-condenar-franquismo/0003_6226393.htm.

Colomer, Josep M. 2020. "Political Institutions in a Comparative Perspective." In *The Oxford Handbook of Spanish Politics*, edited by Diego Muro and Ignacio Lago, 152–70. Oxford, UK: Oxford University Press.

Cortizo, Gonzalo. 2019. "El 72,9% de los votantes del Partido Popular se muestra en contra de sacar a Franco del Valle de los Caídos." *ElDiario.es*, October 16, 2019. https://www. eldiario.es/politica/espanoles-muestran-exhumar-Franco-frente_0_952955653.html.

Cruz Seoane, María, and Susana Sueiro. 2004. *Una historia de* El País *y del Grupo Prisa*. Barcelona: Plaza y Janés.

CTXT. 2020. "Ideas para cambiar de ciclo." *CTXT: Revista Contexto*, January 11, 2020. https://ctxt.es/es/20200108/ Firmas/30490/Editorial-CTXT-gobierno-progresista-ideas-cambio-ciclo.htm.

De Lucas, Miguel. 2017. "El sabio, el tuerto y la esposa del diablo." *CTXT: Revista Contexto*, July 26, 2017. https://ctxt.es/es/20170726/Culturas/14186/

Ctxt-ministerio-Unamuno-Milan-Astray-Franco-Carmen-Polo-Salvador-Vila-Juan-Peset.htm.

Delgado, Luisa Elena. 2014. *La nación singular: La cultura del consenso y la fantasía de normalidad democrática (1999–2011)*. Madrid: Siglo XXI.

Dolgoff, Sam. 1974. *The Anarchist Collectives Workers' Self-Management in the Spanish Revolution, 1936–1939*. New York: Free Life.

Echevarría, Ignacio. 2019. "Apuntes alrededor de 'Mientras dure la guerra.'" *CTXT: Revista Contexto*, November 20, 2019. https://ctxt.es/es/20191120/Culturas/29670/mientras-dure-la-guerra-franquismo-ignacio-echevarria.htm.

EIU. 2019. *Democracy Index 2019: A Year of Democratic Setbacks and Popular Protest: A Report by the Economist Intelligence Unit*. London: Economist Intelligence Unit. http://www.eiu.com/Handlers/WhitepaperHandler.ashx?fi=Democracy-Index-2019.pdf.

ElDiario. 2016. "Albert Rivera: 'Las dictaduras no tienen libertad, pero tienen cierta paz y orden.'" *ElDiario.es*, May 27, 2016. https://www.eldiario.es/politica/Albert-Rivera-dictaduras-libertad-cierta_0_520398115.html.

Elliott, J. H. 2018. *Scots and Catalans: Union and Disunion*. New Haven: Yale University Press.

ElPlural. 2020. "El 21% de los votantes de Vox prefieren una dictadura 'en algunas circunstancias.'" *ElPlural*, January 16, 2020. https://www.elplural.com/politica/espana/21-votantes-vox-prefieren-dictadura-en-circunstancias_231363102.

Encarnación, Omar G. 2014. *Democracy without Justice in Spain: The Politics of Forgetting*. Philadelphia: University of Pennsylvania Press.

———. 2020. "Memory and Politics in Democratic Spain." In *The Oxford Handbook of Spanish Politics*, edited by Diego

Muro and Ignacio Lago, 47–61. Oxford, UK: Oxford University Press.

Escolar, Ignacio, and Raquel Ejerique. 2019. "La intrahistoria de la exhumación de Franco: 'Aquí estamos, abuelo, hemos venido con estos profanadores.'" *ElDiario.es*, October 26, 2019. https://www.eldiario.es/politica/intrahistoria-exhumacion-Franco-abuelo-profanadores_0_956455201.html.

Escudero, Rafael. 2014. "Road to Impunity: The Absence of Transitional Justice Programs in Spain." *Human Rights Quarterly* 36 (1): 123–46.

———. 2013. "The Right to Know: A Foreword." In *Shoot the Messenger? Spanish Democracy and the Crimes of Francoism: From the Pact of Silence to the Trial of Baltasar Garzón*, by Francisco Espinosa Maestre, xii-xxv. Eastbourne: Sussex Academic Press.

Espinosa Maestre, Francisco. 2013. *Shoot the Messenger? Spanish Democracy and the Crimes of Francoism: From the Pact of Silence to the Trial of Baltasar Garzón*. Eastbourne: Sussex Academic Press.

Esteban, Asunción, Dunia Etura, and Matteo Tomasoni, eds. 2019. *La alargada sombra del franquismo: Naturaleza, mecanismos de pervivencia y huellas de la dictadura*. Granada: Comares.

European Commission. 2019a. *The 2019 EU Justice Scoreboard*. Luxembourg: Publications Office of the European Union. https://ec.europa.eu/info/sites/info/files/justice_scoreboard_2019_en.pdf.

———. 2019b. *Standard Eurobarometer 91: Report: Public Opinion in the European Union: Fieldwork June 2019.* https://ec.europa.eu/commfrontoffice/publicopinion/index.cfm/ResultDoc/download/DocumentKy/88420.

Faber, Sebastiaan. 1993. "Geel en rood, Franco is dood." *Strapats*, no. 8 (Winter 1993): 34–37.

——. 2008. "Fantasmas hispanistas y otros retos transatlánticos." In *Cultura y cambio social en América Latina*, edited by Mabel Moraña, 315–45. St Louis, MO: Washington U./Iberoamericana.

——. 2017. "Catalonia Is Real. And Yet . . ." *Public Books*, October 18, 2017. http://www.publicbooks.org/catalonia-is-real-and-yet.

——. 2018. *Memory Battles of the Spanish Civil War: History, Fiction, Photography*. Nashville, TN: Vanderbilt University Press.

——. 2019a. "De grafsteen van Franco om de nek van Spanje." *De Groene Amsterdammer*, November 7, 2019: 12–15. https://www.groene.nl/artikel/de-grafsteen-van-franco-om-de-nek-van-spanje.

——. 2019b. "Fighting the Black Hole: Teaching Twentieth-Century History through Comics." *Volunteer* 36, no. 4 (2019): 5. http://www.albavolunteer.org/2019/12/fighting-the-black-hole-teaching-twentieth-century-history-through-comics-in-spain.

——. 2020. "'Uno de los capítulos más oscuros de la historia reciente': La cultura de la memoria y la imagen del franquismo en los documentales de TV3." In *Con la posguerra en el retrovisor: Las representaciones culturales del período franquista en la democracia española (1975–2019)*, edited by Elizabeth Amann, María Teresa Navarrete, Nettah Yoeli-Rimmer, and Diana Arbaiza, 167–88. Frankfurt: Vervuert.

Faber, Sebastiaan, and Bécquer Seguín. 2015. "The Spanish Media Are the Worst in Europe. These Upstarts Are Trying to Change That." *The Nation*, September 15, 2015. http://www.thenation.com/article/the-spanish-media-are-the-worst-in-europe-these-upstarts-are-trying-to-change-that.

——. 2019. "Media Control and Emancipation: The Public Sphere in Post-15M Spain." In *Spain after the Indignados/15M Movement*, edited by Óscar Pereira-Zazo and Steven L.

Torres, 171–87. New York: Palgrave.

———. 2020. "How the Fight Over Spain's Anti-Fascist Legacy Involves a Former 'Nation' Editor." *The Nation*, December 28, 2020. https://www.thenation.com/article/world/spain-antifa-civil-war.

Faber, Sebastiaan, and Gijs Mulder. 2018. "'Cuando la gente decide cambiar de Estado, eso es irreversible'—Carles Puigdemont, Expresident de la Generalitat." *CTXT: Revista Contexto*, October 3, 2018. https://ctxt.es/es/20181003/Politica/22086/entrevista-carles-puigdemont-republica-catalana-irreversabilidad-proces.htm.

Fallarás, Cristina. 2013. *A la puta calle: Crónica de un desahucio.* Barcelona: Bronce.

Ferrándiz, Francisco. 2014. *El pasado bajo tierra: Exhumaciones contemporáneas de la Guerra Civil.* Barcelona: Anthropos.

Ferrándiz, Francisco, and Tony Robben, ed. 2015. *Necropolitics: Mass Graves and Exhumations in the Age of Human Rights.* Philadelphia: University of Pennsylvania Press.

Field, Bonnie N. 2020. "Legislative Politics in Spain." In *The Oxford Handbook of Spanish Politics*, edited by Diego Muro and Ignacio Lago, 210–23. Oxford, UK: Oxford University Press.

Fontana, Josep. 2012. Prologue. In *Jueces, pero parciales: La pervivencia del franquismo en el poder judicial*, by Carlos Jiménez Villarejo and Antonio Doñate Martín. Barcelona: Pasado y Presente. Kindle.

Forum voor Democratie. 2019a. *De gouden eeuwen van Nederland.* Forum voor Democratie, October 9, 2019. https://forumvoordemocratie.nl/dossiers/gouden-eeuwen.

———. 2019b. *Michiel de Ruyter | De Gouden Eeuwen van Nederland.* Forum voor Democratie, October 6, 2019. YouTube video, https://www.youtube.com/watch?v=4vdEufua5tU.

Franco, Francisco. 1959. "Discurso en la inauguración del Valle de los Caídos." Generalísimo Francisco Franco (website), http://www.generalisimofranco.com/discursos/discursos/1959/00003.htm.

Fuentes, Juan Francisco. 2011. *Adolfo Suárez: Biografía política.* Barcelona: Editorial Planeta.

Gabilondo, Joseba. 2014. "Spanish Nationalist Excess: A Decolonial and Postnational Critique of Iberian Studies." *Prosopopeya: Revista de crítica contemporánea*, no. 8: 23–60.

———. 2019a. *Introduction to a Postnational History of Contemporary Basque Literature (1978–2000): Remnants of a Nation.* London: Tamesis.

———. 2019b. "Posimperialismo, estudios ibéricos y enfoques comparativo-sistémicos: Pornografía neoliberal española, terrorismo antropológico-turístico y oasis vasco." In *Perspectivas críticas sobre os estudios ibéricos*, edited by Cristina Martínez Tejero and Santiago Pérez Isasi, 88–112. Biblioteca di *Rassegna iberistica*. Venice: Edizioni Ca'Foscari.

Garcés, Joan E. 2012. *Soberanos e intervenidos: Estrategias globales, americanos y españoles.* 4th ed. Madrid: Siglo XXI.

Garoupa, Nuno, and Pedro C. Magalhães. 2020. "Judicial Politics: The Constitutional Court." In *The Oxford Handbook of Spanish Politics*, edited by Diego Muro and Ignacio Lago, 258–75. Oxford, UK: Oxford University Press.

Gay, Nacho. 2019. "España sigue siendo monárquica gracias a los andaluces y a pesar de catalanes y vascos." *Vanitatis el confidencial*, June 19, 2019. https://www.vanitatis.elconfidencial.com/casas-reales/2019-06-19/encuesta-vanitatis-felipe-letizia-monarquia-republica-espana-cataluna_2075143.

Graham, Helen. 2012. *The War and Its Shadow: Spain's Civil War in Europe's Long Twentieth Century.* Brighton: Sussex

Academic Press.

———. 2005. *The Spanish Civil War: A Very Short Introduction*. Oxford, UK: Oxford University Press.

Greenberg, Jon. 2015. "Bernie Sanders: U.S. 'Only Major Country' That Doesn't Guarantee Right to Health Care." *Politifact*, June 29, 2015. https://www.politifact.com/factchecks/2015/jun/29/bernie-s/bernie-sanders-us-only-major-country-doesnt-guaran.

Hernández Sánchez, Fernando. 2014. *El bulldozer negro del General Franco: Historia de España en el Siglo XX para la primera generación del XXI*. Barcelona: Pasado & Presente.

Hierro, María José. 2020. "Regional and National Identities in Spain." In *The Oxford Handbook of Spanish Politics*, edited by Diego Muro and Ignacio Lago, 494–509. Oxford, UK: Oxford University Press.

Horowitz, David. 2006. *The Professors: The 101 Most Dangerous Academics in America*. Washington, DC: Regnery.

Hristova, Marije. 2016. *Reimagining Spain: Transnational Entanglements and Remembrance of the Spanish Civil War since 1989*. PhD diss., Universitaire Pers Maastricht.

Humlebæk, Carsten. 2015. *Spain: Inventing the Nation*. London: Bloomsbury.

Intereconomía (@eltorotv). 2020. "Los comunistas que provocaron la Guerra Civil vuelven al Gobierno." Twitter, January 9, 2020, 5:30 a.m. https://twitter.com/Intereconomia/status/1215234337903448065

Izquierdo Martín, Jesús, and Pablo Sánchez León. 2006. *La guerra que nos han contado: 1936 y nosotros*. Madrid: Alianza.

Jiménez, David. 2019. *El director: Secretos e intrigas de la prensa narrados por el exdirector de* El Mundo. Madrid: Libros del K.O. Kindle.

Jiménez Villarejo, Carlos, and Antonio Doñate Martín. 2012. *Jueces, pero parciales: La pervivencia del franquismo en el poder judicial*. Barcelona: Pasado y Presente. Kindle.

Juliá, Santos. 2017. *Transición: Historia de una política española (1937–2017)*. Madrid: Galaxia Gutenberg.

Junquera, Natalia. 2013. "Víctimas del franquismo denuncian a un diputado del PP por injurias." *El País*, November 25, 2013. https://elpais.com/politica/2013/11/25/actualidad/1385409942_108975.html.

———. 2019. "El CIS da un cómodo triunfo al PSOE, que dobla al PP en escaños el 28-A." *El País*, April 9, 2019. https://elpais.com/politica/2019/04/09/actualidad/1554791390_073854.html.

Kaufman, Dan. 2012. "A Judge in the Dock." *New York Times* 25 Jan. http://www.nytimes.com/2012/01/26/opinion/in-spain-baltasar-garzon-on-trial.html.

Larraz, Fernando. 2009. *El monopolio de la palabra: El exilio intelectual en la España franquista*. Madrid: Biblioteca Nueva.

———. 2014. *Letricidio español: Censura y novela durante el franquismo*. Gijón: Trea.

LaSexta. 2016a. "Rajoy: 'Me gustaría que se supiera dónde están enterrados sus abuelos pero no tengo claro que pueda hacer nada el Gobierno.'" *Salvados*, April 3, 2016. https://www.lasexta.com/programas/salvados/mejores-momentos/rajoy-gustaria-que-supiera-donde-estan-enterrados-sus-abuelos-pero-tengo-claro-que-pueda-hacer-nada-gobierno_20160403572383866584a81fd881e73f.html.

———. 2016b. "Así confesó Adolfo Suárez por qué no hubo referéndum monarquía o república: 'Hacíamos encuestas y perdíamos.'" *La sexta columna*, November 18, 2016. https://www.lasexta.com/programas/sexta-columna/noticias/asi-confeso-adolfo-suarez-por-que-no-hubo-referendum-monarquia-o-republica-haciamos-encuestas-y-perdiamos_201611185 82ef9feocf244336fo9709f.html.

————. 2017. "Cantan el 'Cara al sol' en el funeral por el exministro franquista Utrera Molina frente a Ruiz-Gallardón." *Noticias*, April 23, 2017. https://www.lasexta.com/noticias/nacional/cantan-el-cara-al-sol-en-el-funeral-por-el-exministro-franquista-utrera-molina-al-que-acudio-ruiz-gallardon_201704235 8fc70f60cf2ea95b02b2080.html.

————. 2019. "Un 37,4% de votantes del PP y un 58,5% de los de Vox creen que Franco no fue un dictador." *Barómetro de LaSexta*, October 24, 2019. https://www.lasexta.com/noticias/nacional/barometro-lasexta-un-374-de-votantes-del-pp-y-un-585-de-los-de-vox-creen-que-franco-no-fue-un-dictador_201910245db1600c0cf2d4f059b98a13.html.

————. 2020. "Las polémicas proclamas de los manifestantes de Vox." *El Intermedio*, January 13, 2020. https://www.atresplayer.com/lasexta/programas/el-intermedio/clips/franco-salvo-espana-o-puede-ocurrir-otra-guerra-civil-las-polemicas-proclamas-de-los-asistentes-a-la-manifestacion-de-vox_5e1cf72c7ed1a8c0b487b663.

Maestre, Antonio. 2019a. *Franquismo, S.A.* Madrid: Akal. Kindle.

————. 2019b. "Un día de la vergüenza." *La Marea*, October 24, 2019. https://www.lamarea.com/2019/10/24/exhumacion-de-franco-dia-verguenza.

Martín Pallín, José Antonio, and Rafael Escudero, eds. 2008. *Derecho y memoria histórica.* Madrid: Trotta.

Martínez, Guillem, ed. 2012. *CT, o, La cultura de la Transición: Crítica a 35 años de cultura española.* Barcelona: Random House Mondadori.

Martínez, Guillem. 2016. *La gran ilusión: Mito y realidad del proceso indepe.* Madrid: Debate.

Mercado, Francisco. 1992. "El acto central del 20-N revela la división interna en el seno de la ultraderecha." *El País,*

November 23, 1992. https://elpais.com/diario/1992/11/23/
espana/722473216_850215.html.

Minder, Raphael. 2017. *The Struggle for Catalonia: Rebel Politics
in Spain*. London: Hurst.

Monforte Jaén, Marta. 2018. "Todas las veces en las que el
PP ha rechazado condenar el franquismo en el Congreso."
Público, November 21, 2018. https://www.publico.es/
politica/veces-pp-rechazado-condenar-franquismo.html.

Moret, Xavier. 1992. "El franquismo era feísimo; daba la
impresión de que a todo el mundo le olían los calcetines."
El País, October 26, 1992, 26. https://elpais.com/
diario/1992/10/26/cultura/720054002_850215.html.

Núñez Seixas, Xosé M. 2018. *Suspiros de España: El nacionalismo
español, 1808–2018*. Barcelona: Crítica.

———. 2020. "Spanish Nationalism since 1975." In *The Oxford
Handbook of Spanish Politics*, edited by Diego Muro and
Ignacio Lago, 479–93. Oxford, UK: Oxford University
Press.

Osiris. 2020. Reader's comment to Rosa María Artal, "Un
fascismo impregnado de franquismo y estulticia." *ElDiario.
es*, January 17, 2020. https://www.eldiario.es/zonacritica/
fascismo-impregnado-franquismo-estulticia_6_985911416.
html.

Pardo Torregrosa, Iñaki. 2020. "Azaña, el arma arrojadiza
en el Congreso." *La Vanguardia*, January 7, 2020. https://
www.lavanguardia.com/politica/20200107/472770586477/
manuel-azana-disputa-congreso-diputados-debate-
investidura-pedro-sanchez-casado-abascal-arrimadas.html.

Payne, Stanley. 2019. *En defensa de España: Desmontando mitos y
leyendas negras*. Barcelona: Planeta.

Pérez, Claudi. 2020. "Junqueras: 'El apoyo a los Presupuestos
depende de los avances en la mesa de diálogo.'" *El País*,

January 18, 2020. https://elpais.com/politica/2020/01/17/actualidad/1579285478_146900.html.

President's Advisory 1776 Commission. 2021. *The 1776 Report*. Washington, DC: President's Advisory 1776 Commission.

Preston, Paul. 1994. *Franco: A Biography*. New York: Basic Books.

———. 2012. *The Spanish Holocaust: Inquisition and Extermination in Twentieth-Century Spain*. New York: Norton.

———. 2020. *A People Betrayed: A History of Corruption, Political Incompetence and Social Division in Modern Spain*. London: Liveright.

Reuters. 2015. *Reuters Digital News Report 2015*. Oxford: Reuters Institute for the Study of Journalism; University of Oxford. https://reutersinstitute.politics.ox.ac.uk/sites/default/files/research/files/Reuters%2520Institute%2520Digital%2520News%2520Report%25202015_Full%2520Report.pdf.

Reyes Guzmán, Eduardo. 2012. "The European People's Party (EPP) Did Not Condemn the Dictatorship of Francisco Franco." European Parliament, August 17, 2012. YouTube video, https://www.youtube.com/watch?v=7yjzX4OUgTM.

Richards, Michael. 1998. *A Time of Silence: Civil War and the Culture of Repression in Franco's Spain, 1936–1945*. Cambridge, UK: Cambridge University Press.

———. 2013. *After the Civil War: Making Memory and Re-making Spain since 1936*. Cambridge, UK: Cambridge University Press.

Riveiro, Aitor, and Mario Escribano. 2018. "Los hijos del franquista Utrera Molina alegan que llamarle 'asesino' por firmar penas de muerte atenta contra su honor." *ElDiario.es*, July 11, 2018. https://www.eldiario.es/politica/

franquista-Utrera-Molina-denuncian-Rufian_0_791621350.
html.

Roca Barea, María Elvira. 2016. *Imperiofobia y leyenda negra: Roma, Rusia, Estados Unidos y el Imperio español*. Madrid: Siruela.

———. 2019. *Fracasología: España y sus elites*. Barcelona: Planeta.

Rocha, Carlos. 2019. "Multa de 5.000 euros a Teresa Rodríguez por llamar asesino a Utrera Molina." *Diario de Sevilla*, May 20, 2019. https://www.diariodesevilla.es/andalucia/Multa-Teresa-Rodriguez-Utrera-Molina_0_1356464535.html.

Rodríguez, Jesús. 2019. "Entramos en el laberinto de los secretos de Estado en España." *El País Semanal*, December 27, 2019. https://elpais.com/elpais/2019/12/27/eps/1577459032_834241.html.

Rodríguez, Teresa (@TeresaRodr_). 2018. "Hoy hace 44 años de la ejecución a garrote vil de Salvador Puig Antich." Twitter, March 2, 2018, 1:09 p.m. https://twitter.com/TeresaRodr_/status/969650965333925888.

Roures i Lop, Jaume, dir. 2017. *Las cloacas de interior*. Barcelona: MediaPro.

Ruiz, Julius. 2015. *The "Red Terror" and the Spanish Civil War: Revolutionary Violence in Madrid*. Cambridge, UK: Cambridge University Press.

Ruptly. 2019. "Spain: Vox Leader Draws on Reconquista for Campaign Launch." Ruptly, April 12, 2019. YouTube video, https://www.youtube.com/watch?v=8xCLOgVNYMs.

RTVE. 2020. "Intervención íntegra de Mertxe Aizpurua (EH Bildu) en el debate de investidura." RTVE, January 5, 2020. https://www.rtve.es/alacarta/videos/especiales-informativos/intervencion-integra-mertxe-aizpurua-eh-bildu-debate-investidura/5477557.

Sanclemente, José. 2015. "El control político de los medios de comunicación." *ElDiario.es*, 16 July 2015. https://www.

eldiario.es/opinion/zona-critica/control-politico-medios-comunicacion_129_2566732.html.

Sánchez-Cuenca, Ignacio. 2020. "Spanish Democratization: Transition, Consolidation, and its Meaning in Contemporary Spain." In *The Oxford Handbook of Spanish Politics*, edited by Diego Muro and Ignacio Lago, 32–46. Oxford, UK: Oxford University Press.

Seidman, Michael. 2011. *The Victorious Counterrevolution: The Nationalist Effort in the Spanish Civil War*. Madison: University of Wisconsin Press.

Serrano, Pascual. 2010. *Traficantes de información: La historia oculta de los grupos de comunicación españoles*. Madrid: Akal.

———. 2012. *Periodismo Canalla: Los medios contra la información*. Madrid: Icaria.

Shubert, Adrian, and José Álvarez Junco. 2000. Introduction to *Spanish History since 1808*, edited by Adrian Shubert and José Álvarez Junco. London: Arnold.

Silva, Emilio. 2019. "Exhumar al dictador: Y romper el concordato de la democracia con el franquismo." *ElDiario.es*, September 24, 2019. https://www.eldiario.es/tribunaabierta/Exhumar-dictador-concordato-democracia-franquismo_6_945665467.html.

Straehle, Edgar. 2019. "Historia y leyenda de la Leyenda Negra (I): El retorno de la leyenda negra y Roca Barea." *Conversación sobre historia*, July 21, 2019. https://conversacionsobrehistoria.info/2019/07/21/historia-y-leyenda-de-la-leyenda-negra-i-el-retorno-de-la-leyenda-negra-y-roca-barea.

Torrús, Alejandro. 2017. "Los Franco, una inmensa fortuna que arrancó con una gran matanza fundacional." *Público*, December 29, 2017. https://www.publico.es/politica/franco-inmensa-fortuna-arranco-gran-matanza-fundacional.html.

Tremlett, Giles. 2007. *Ghosts of Spain: Travels through Spain and Its Silent Past*. London: Walker Books.

Tribunal Supremo. 2012. "Sentencia No. 101/2012." Tribunal Supremo. Sala de lo Penal, February 27, 2012. http://ww.elconfidencial.com/archivos/ec/2012022778sentenciagarzon.doc.

TV3. 2019. "Manuel Castells: 'El problema és la frustració de la gent i, en particular, dels joves.'" *Preguntes Freqüents*, October 26, 2019. https://www.ccma.cat/tv3/alacarta/preguntes-frequents/manuel-castells-el-problema-es-la-frustracio-de-la-gent-i-en-particular-dels-joves/video/5946567.

United Nations Human Rights Committee. 2015. "Concluding Observations on the Sixth Periodic Report of Spain." CCPR/C/ESP/CO/6 New York: UNO, August 14, 2015. http://tbinternet.ohchr.org/_layouts/treatybodyexternal/Download.aspx?symbolno=CCPR%2fC%2fESP%2fCO%2f6&Lang=en.

Univers. 2019. "Baudet: 'We worden ondermijnd door onze universiteiten.'" *Univers: The Independent News Source of Tilburg University*, March 21, 2019. https://universonline.nl/2019/03/21/baudet-worden-ondermijnd-door-onze-universiteiten.

Urbán Crespo, Miguel (@MiguelUrban). 2019. "Imagináis a un juez condenando a alguien." Twitter, May 20, 2019, 3:56 p.m. https://twitter.com/MiguelUrban/status/1130578040180891649.

Urías, Joaquín (@jpurias). 2019. "Esto es intolerable." Twitter, May 20, 2019. https://twitter.com/jpurias/status/1130447849341235200.

Vanguardia. 2019a. "UE: España debe analizar por qué hay menos confianza en el poder judicial." *La Vanguardia*, April 26, 2019. https://www.lavanguardia.com/vida/20190426/461872140597/ue-espana-debe-analizar-por-que-hay-menos-confianza-en-el-poder-judicial.html.

————. 2019b. "Abascal, éxtasis ante Don Pelayo." *La Vanguardia*, April 12, 2019. https://www.lavanguardia.com/politica/20190412/461603055367/vox-covadonga-asturias-don-pelayo-elecciones-28a.html.

Vázquez Montalbán, Manuel. 1992. *Autobiografía del general Franco*. Barcelona: Planeta.

Villacañas, José Luis. 2019. *Imperiofilia y el populismo nacional-católico: Otra historia del imperio español*. Madrid: Lengua de Trapo.

Viñas, Ángel. 2015. *La otra cara del caudillo: Mitos y realidades en la biografía de Franco*. Barcelona: Crítica.

Vinyes, Ricard. 2002. *Irredentas: Las presas políticas y sus hijos en las cárceles franquistas*. Madrid: Temas de Hoy.

————. 2009. "La memoria del Estado." In *El estado y la memoria*, 23–66. Madrid: RBA.

————. 2019. "Apología de la ruina." *Público*, December 11, 2019. https://blogs.publico.es/otrasmiradas/26551/apologia-de-la-ruina.

Volunteer. "Vet Pees Homage." *Volunteer* 25, no. 3 (Sept. 2003): 3.

Vox España. 2018. "Discurso de Santiago Abascal en Vistalegre." Vox España, October 7, 2018. YouTube video, https://www.youtube.com/watch?v=t_CIfZ5amIE.

INDEX

9 780826 501738